A gift for

Natalie

From Grandma & Grandpa Phil

To Natalie

Keep on being

Amazing

Best Wishes

Linda Finstad

on the occassion of your 14th birthday.

The everyday angels featured in this book were
created for your delight and entertainment
by Linda Finstad.
What makes the illustrations both unique and amazing is that
Linda painted them using coffee instead of paint.

ISBN 978-1-990553-01-1

The Art of Being
Amazing

Within every girl there is a princess with the spirit of a warrior.

You don't have to be perfect
to be amazing!

Subjects:

Dedicated to
my younger self.

I wish someone had given me this book years ago.
It would have eliminated so much wasted time trying to please others by trying to be something I was clearly not.
I could have stepped into my amazing life much sooner.

Also dedicated to my darling daughter, Kate,
(who is already amazing).

Why settle for "fine" or "just OK" when you have the potential to be **Amazing.** To simplify - there is good, there is great and there is **Amazing.**

The good news is, you don't have to be rich or famous to be amazing. In fact everything you need to know is right here in the pages of this book.

Before we dive into the secret sauce of being amazing let's define what being amazing really means.

A Google search revealed:

Amazing, like incredible, awesome, and fabulous, is used so often to describe things that are really good, you sometimes forget that its real meaning is reserved for things that are especially remarkable. The base word in amazing is amaze, which means "to astound or perplex." So amazing should be reserved for things that do just that. Things that are extremely impressive or surprisingly great; inspiring awe.

Synonyms: breathtaking, awesome, stunning, astounding, astonishing, awe-inspiring, stupendous, staggering, extraordinary, incredible, unbelievable, magnificent, wonderful, spectacular, remarkable, phenomenal, prodigious, miraculous, sublime, formidable, imposing, impressive, mind-boggling, mind-blowing, out-of-this world, amaze-balls, bad-ass, wondrous.

By striving to become more amazing than you already are, you will open the door to the abundance of possibilities that come with putting out awesome vibes into the world. Your luck will improve and good things will start coming and happening to you on a regular basis.

I will use the words awesome and amazing to describe the way of life that is freely available to you. Living an amazing life is all about how you behave and interact in the world. It's about being your greatest self and putting yourself and what you have to offer out into the world. Being amazing is waking up each morning with the intention of moving forward on your journey, progressing as a person, and wanting to do whatever you can to make a positive difference in your life and the lives of others.

I will freely admit, learning the secret of how to be amazing and live an awesome life has been a somewhat selfish quest. However, I am thrilled to share my findings with you, so you too, can master the art of being amazing.

There are no classes at school on how to think, yet we emerge from high school with the ability to form opinions on a whole host of things. We have a code of conduct and an understanding of what is right and wrong. We even think we know who we are.
So who taught us how to think?

This might seem like a silly question and perhaps one you have never considered before, but I urge you to take a moment and think back to who influenced your thinking as you moved through childhood toward adulthood.

Who taught you how to think and what if they got it wrong?

If you are like most people it was your parents who taught you how to think about the world around you. They taught you from a very early age what was acceptable and polite behavior, what was right and what was wrong. They would have introduced you to whatever religion or spiritual belief they practiced and as a child you would have accepted this way of thinking as normal and followed their lead.

Your parents would have been taught to think by their parents in much the same way. And their parents by their parents. This is one explanation as to why family feuds carry on for generations, long after the reason for the feud has been forgotten.

You may have won the genetic lottery and been born into a family with parents who encouraged you to explore all options and become all that you could be. If this was the case you may be familiar with phrases such as:

You are loved and I am proud of you.
You are creative.
Trust your instincts, because your ideas are worth-while.
You can learn from your mistakes.
You can do or be anything if you work hard enough.
Never say you can't do something until you have given it your best shot.
Your ideas are interesting.
You've made me think of things in a completely new way.
I'm excited to see what you do.

Your parents may have encouraged you to respect others with phrases like:
You don't have to like what someone is saying in order to treat them with respect.
Everyone is entitled to their own opinion, just as you are entitled to yours.
Someone else's poor behavior is not an excuse for your own.

The way we talk to our kids becomes their inner voice.

One piece of encouraging advice my father gave to me that has stayed with me all my life was this:
You can have anything you want in life - if you want it badly enough and are prepared to do whatever it takes to get it. My father never said we could not afford it or that I could not have something. I am not saying he gave me everything I ever asked for (in fact the opposite was true), but he always filled me with the hope that I could have whatever I wanted in life just as long as I wanted it badly enough and was prepared to do whatever it took.

Of course, there are many more words of encouragement that you may have heard as a child that helped form your self-esteem and build your confidence to try new things and be all you could possibly be.

Unfortunately, the same is also true of negative comments that are made by parents that seem to have an even greater, more lasting effect on the way a child learns to think about themselves, the people around them and the world.

There are statements such as:
We can't afford it - money doesn't grow on trees. This instills a belief that there is not enough to go around.

Don't talk to strangers. Of course the parents' intention was to keep their children from interacting with dangerous individuals. However it also conveys to a small child that everyone who is not immediate family is bad.

Stop crying - don't be such a baby - you are fine. This makes children feel like they are wrong for showing emotion. We probably all know guys who are incapable of expressing their feelings because they were taught from an early age to hide those feelings.

You did well, but you could do better. This negative compliment makes children feel like they are not quite good enough for their parents to be proud of them.

"Because I said so." or "Because I'm an adult and you're a child."
The my-way-or-the-highway approach may have been one used for a very long time, but that does not make it the right way to discipline children. It also makes children feel like their opinions aren't valid simply because they are young.

"I wish you were more like............... A child's self-esteem can really take a knock when they are told this. Whether they are compared to a sibling, or anyone else for that matter, it makes them feel like they are not enough.

I am sure you can think of many more examples but I had to stop because to be honest it's quite depressing. The good news is that, you can choose what phrases to say to yourself and the more you say them to yourself the more you will believe them to be true.

Positive thinking can only get you so far.

It is essential that we don't get caught up in only thinking positively. You can sit in the garden of your mind telling yourself there are no weeds, but to build a truly fulfilling life, you need to stop covering up the weeds with positive thinking – and pick them instead.

I am a firm believer in the power of positive thinking, however to achieve anything worth having requires action. Sitting around thinking about learning to swim won't make you a swimmer. If you want to learn to swim it requires putting on a swimsuit and actually getting into the water.

Most amazing people choose to think positively.
This might seem a simplistic approach and I am not saying the secret sauce to achieving a happy and amazing life is to just think positively, but it is a choice. When you choose to view life and circumstances in a positive light, life is infinitely better.

The simplest test is to determine if you are a positive thinker or not is to listen to how you talk about the weather. Discussing the weather is probably the most common topic of conversation around the world. Regardless of where you live or your ethnic background complaining about the weather is a topic that spans the universe.

Which of these statements describes how you talk about the weather?

Do you say? "Oh no! What a dreadful day. It's raining again."
Or do you say, "The garden is going to look fabulous with all this rain."

Do you say? "It's a beautiful sunny day - perfect for a picnic."
Or do you complain that the UV rays will be dangerous today, so we'd better stay indoors.

Do you say? "I hate dark foggy mornings."
Or do you love to watch the mist rise in the morning as it makes the world look so mysterious.

Train your brain to see the good in everything. Positivity is a choice.
Your amazing life depends on the quality of your thoughts.

Positive thinking really is a choice.
If you catch yourself thinking negatively about something, challenge yourself to think of the opposite, positive alternative.

There have been many studies to prove that positive thinking also has a positive impact on your physical and mental health.

Some physical benefits may include:

Longer life span
Lower chance of having a heart attack
Better physical health
Greater resistance to illness such as the common cold
Lower blood pressure
Better stress management
Better pain tolerance

The mental benefits may include:

More creativity
Greater problem-solving skill
Clearer thinking
Better mood,
Better coping skills
Less depression

How amazing is that?.

The magic begins when you believe in yourself.
If you can do that, you can make anything happen.

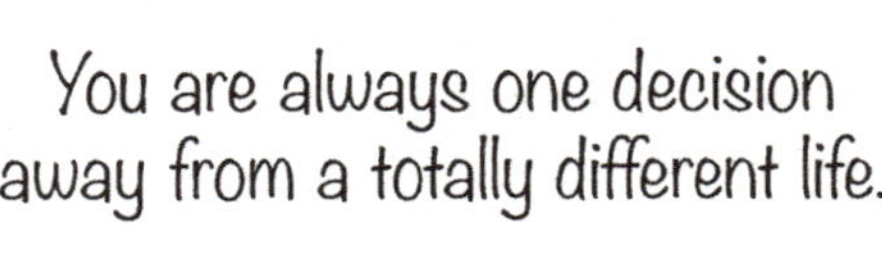

It is true to say positive thinking won't achieve anything, but it is also true that positive thinking will help you to do everything better than negative thinking will.

Positive thinking allows you to access all the abilities, gifts and talents that you already have inside of you, which is awesome.

It works like turning on a tap. When you turn on a tap the water flows out.
Turning the tap did not generate the water, it merely allowed it to flow.
The water was already stored and waiting to be released.
Positive thinking works the same way.

Creativity is thinking up new things.
Innovation is doing new things.

To get your positive thinking juices flowing try answering the following questions:

1.What would you do if the world was going to end one week from today?
2. Look back on your life and think about the three most important lessons you learned and why they had such an impact on you.
3. Think of someone who inspires you. What exactly is it that they do that makes you feel amazing when in their presence?
4. List 10 things that you really appreciate, but that you take for granted.
5. It's your 99th birthday and friends and family are gathered and invited to say a few words about you - what do you want them to say?
6. What surprising things have surfaced in your awareness by answering these questions?

A strong woman knows she has strength enough for the journey.
But a woman of strength knows it is in the journey
where she will become strong.

Wimp or Wonder Woman

We can't all be heroes with super human powers, but we can all increase our awesomeness by making incremental changes to our habits and beliefs. The good news is you have everything you need to make these changes already inside you.

To get you in the right frame of mind I want you to set a big, audacious, daring goal. Something that you think is maybe out of your reach or capability and start taking steps to make it happen. With each step you take in the direction of your daring, audacious goal you will become more awesome.

The trouble with not having a clear goal is that you can spend your life running up and down the field and never score.

I confessed earlier that writing this book was a selfish act to release my own inner awesomeness. If I am to suggest ways to become more amazing and live an awesome life I had better test some of these theories, so, I decided to put this step to the test.

I am an artist and author and my big audacious goal is to become famous. Hmmm….. I pondered long and hard on how I would make this happen, then I remembered the process is to take small steps in the direction of the goal, so my first step was to name it and claim it. I bought the domain name FamousCoffeeArtist.com and added this to my website. This was a bold step and one that made me cringe a little at the audacity of posting this claim on the internet, but after a couple of days that feeling passed and I started planning the next step towards my goal.

Maybe you have a big, bold, audacious goal or perhaps you had one in the past that you let go. Take a moment to write it down. **The bolder the better**

I know big, bold moves towards being amazing can be intimidating and to be honest a little scary so let's ease into this process a little at a time.

If we don't feel happy with what we already have.
What makes us think we would be happy with more of the same.

How do I know if I have lost my Mojo?

If you are feeling depleted, overwhelmed, stressed-out, frumpy, tired, bored or lethargic, you may have lost your Mojo. Once lost, it is really hard to find the motivation to reclaim it. But you can't remain in that Mojo-less place for too long, apathy could mushroom into an even worse state of mind.

Take this little quiz.

If you answer yes to most of the following questions there is a good chance you have lost your Mojo.

1. Are you constantly feeling tired and your quality me time, is just nap time?

2. Do you wander around craft stores looking for inspiration and perhaps a new hobby that you can feel excited about?

3. Do you feel dissatisfied with your life even though nothing fundamental has changed?

4. You know fresh air and exercise is supposed to be invigorating and will help you to feel energized, but even the thought of exercise is exhausting.

5. Are you bored with all the things and activities that once gave you pleasure.

6. Would you prefer to eat take-out, alone in your pj's, than cook up a fancy meal and invite people over?

7. Do you ever look at your life and think "is this it"?

8. Do you cut your own hair and regard manicures as a waste of money ?

9. Have you been struggling to take off that last 10 pounds (or 20 pounds) for more than six months?

10. Have you given up on the dreams of your youth because you believe it's never going to happen. I am probably too old now anyway?

Your missing Mojo might also be attributed to other factors such as;
The kids have left home and you are feeling as if no one really needs you anymore.
You may have been laid off work or retired - this can be challenging and a period of adjustment may be needed. Or a relationship might have ended this could be a romantic relationship or even a close friendship .

This all seems quite depressing so I won't pose any more missing Mojo questions.

Find your missing
Mojo.

I'm not telling you it is easy.
I am telling you it is worth it.

How do I get my Mojo going?
What if my Mojo already got up and left?

I love to do research (I am kind of a geek) so I went in search of the official definition of Mojo. I found many variations ranging from the sexual prowess of Austin Powers to an African magic bag containing a hex. However, the middle ground and probably the most accepted meaning is someone who is charismatic and attracts good fortune. They feel lucky. So how do you get it back if your Mojo has wandered off?

The answer is simple. You fake it till you make it.

When I was a little girl my parents owned the village store. This was the central hub of our village and we sold everything from newspapers to potatoes. As a family business everyone in the family was involved in running the day-to-day operations of the store, including me. I was 12 years old which made me old enough to serve customers and stock shelves. There was a firm rule - when a customer came into the shop - you put aside any personal problems you might be experiencing, you straightened your back, put a smile on your face and greeted the customer with a warm welcome. No complaining, no sulking and certainly no objections. To a lot of kids these days this may seem like child labor and abuse, however it taught me a fabulous lesson on how to fake it.

This may seem like a very simple example of how to be amazing, but think for a moment about the celebrities you admire or athletes who dazzle you with their physical abilities. When it is time for them to step into the spotlight and shine they know they have to bring their "A" game. They perhaps have a similar rule to the one I learned as a child - straighten your back, hold your head up high, stick a smile on your face and show the world you are amazing.

There are a few things people with Mojo do that you can easily copy to resurrect your Mojo.

Imagine the world is your runway.
Go strut your stuff.

Walk with a spring in your step.

People with Mojo use their body language to exude confidence and awesomeness. Try adding a little wiggle to your walk.

Believe you are lucky.

Most of us are luckier than we think.

If you are reading this book you were lucky enough to be born into a family who had the means and ability to provide you with an education. Not everyone in the world is so lucky. And it really is luck, because you had no control over the home you were born into.

When you believe yourself to be a lucky person - you are more open to see opportunities and the good that surrounds you and that is amazing.

Stack the odds in your favor and you are more likely to win and succeed.

I don't mean find a way to rig the lottery or cheat at the blackjack tables, however you can rig the game of life in your favor and set yourself up for success. Consider this scenario. How amazing would it be if your morning was stress free, imagine the kids all were dressed and ready to leave for school with time to spare and everyone in the house started their day relaxed, smiling and eager to face whatever came their way. OK, I am not suggesting you move to Walton's Mountain and John-Boy helps with all the morning chores.

What I am suggesting is stacking the odds in such a way to make this blissful morning a reality. All it needs is a little pre-planning and perhaps re-setting not only your own, but everyones' alarm clocks to allow an extra 20 minutes first thing in the morning. Try making a list of all the things that would make life go more smoothly and then make a second list of ways you could make that happen.

PS. You don't have to do everything yourself - you can include others to help you.

You can't change the world without getting your hands dirty.

One of my morning stresses was packing a lunch for my 6-year-old daughter and more importantly one she would actually eat. So we sat down together and made a list of all the things she liked. Then I asked her to help me plan her lunches for the week and we made a chart that hung on the fridge. This really helped solve two problems. Number One, I had a shopping list of items to help me when I went grocery shopping and Number Two, my daughter actually ate her lunch because she was involved in the planning process. It was a win-win.

Set yourself up for small victories and you will feel like a winner.

Earlier we talked about setting big, bold, audacious goals however it is important to also have small easy-to-achieve goals to boost your confidence along the way. These can be small steps towards your big goal or smaller unrelated tasks. Think of tasks like finishing a novel, or writing a letter or just completing something on your to-do list that has gone from one to-do list to the next. You know what I mean! There is always one job you procrastinate over and leave till last and we justify it by telling ourselves we will do it tomorrow.

Stop whining and complaining.

None of us like to think of ourselves as whiners and complainers and it is easy to think of that one person who is. It is an easy habit to fall into and one you really need to nip in the bud if you want to get your Mojo back. If there's something in your life that you don't like, either try to fix it or move away from it. While it's fine to vent occasionally, endless rumination on the negative is a surefire way to kill your Mojo.

Use body language and cross the finish line like a winner.

Seriously, try this and you will be amazed at how your mood and Mojo soar.
You may want to try this when you are alone and in the privacy of your own front room, but this is what you do: Raise your hands high above your head (just like those runners do as they push their chest against the tape at the finish line of a foot race) and gently run around the room chanting at the top of your voice "I am a winner, I am a winner" .
I know it sounds ridiculous - but it works. Go on - give it a try.

Do something you're good at.
The self-assurance you feel while doing something you're good at will boost your self-esteem and give you the confidence to tackle something new.

Put on your favorite outfit and strut your stuff.

Even if you don't have anywhere special to go, looking good will help you to feel good. Also, spritz on some perfume or cologne. Then call a friend and meet for coffee and bask in the compliments as she raves about how amazing you look.

Be true to yourself.

Nothing will kill your Mojo faster than comparing yourself to others.

Are you doing what you really want to do, or are you trying to fulfill the expectations of others? Are you following conventional wisdom instead of listening to your gut?

Are you letting others make decisions for you? Only you know what's best for you. Trust your inner voice. Paying attention to your authentic needs and listening to your inner wisdom is one of the best ways to get your Mojo back.

Move on and let go of what you can't change.
If your Mojo is down due to a failed relationship, forgive and forget. You can't undo what happened, but you can stop dragging it around with you by refusing to think about it.

Follow a Mojo master.
We all know someone who exudes lots of self-confidence; they always seem happy and upbeat no matter what is going on in their lives. It can be quite annoying especially if we are going through a rough patch. The trick is to model their behavior. They say imitation is the best form of flattery and they obviously are onto something so follow their lead.

If people are going to stare make it worth their while.

Think, world domination.

When my daughter was little she watched a cute cartoon on TV called Pinky and The Brain, featuring two genetically enhanced laboratory mice. Every episode featured one of Brain's attempts at world domination. In every single episode, The Brain failed. However, nothing seemed to discourage The Brain. In every episode there would be the following dialogue.

Pinky, "Gee, Brain, what do you want to do tonight?"
The Brain: "The same thing we do every night, Pinky—try to take over the world!"
It became a little joke in my house when anyone asked the question "what are you doing?" The response was "Trying to take over the world." It was always said in jest but a much more positive and fun answer to the typical response, "Oh nothing."

Be curious and open to new experiences.
Learn something new, find new interests, meet new people, experiment by trying new foods. Unless you have tried something at least once - how do you know if you like it or not? Although I have to say I am prepared to trust my gut on a few things. I am pretty sure I won't like chocolate covered ants or skydiving.

Go outside and get some sun.
Sunlight is vital to your body's ability to produce Vitamin D. Did you know that Vitamin D is not actually a vitamin, but a steroid hormone (the happy hormone) which boosts your mood and increases your energy levels. Let your Mojo in by opening a window or taking a stroll in the park.

Start by doing what is necessary, then do what is possible
and suddenly you are doing the impossible.

Play to your strengths and stack the odds in your favor.

We are all gifted in different ways. There will be certain endeavors, tasks and projects that you find easy to accomplish and some that seem incredibly hard or nigh-on impossible. Personally, I have always been able to draw, this was evident even as a small child. Some would call it a gift or a natural artistic ability. Art and creative projects always came easily to me. However, I am tone deaf and can't even hum in tune; I was definitely at the back of the line when musical talents were being handed out.

This chapter is dedicated to stacking the odds in your favor by playing to your strengths. I am sure you have heard the saying that you can't fit a square peg into a round hole. The same is true of people and the sooner you accept and embrace the concept that it is impossible to be good at everything, the happier and more amazing you will be.

My question to you is: why struggle when you can shine?
The first step is to clarify what your strengths are. Identify and list all the things you are naturally good at and find a way to apply them in your daily life both at home and at work.

Success is achieved
by developing our strengths,
not eliminating our weaknesses.

Make a list of all your strengths and I mean an exhaustive list. Include things that you may think of as trivial. For example, you may be good with children. Jotting that down would be a great start, but expand on that quality to include possible other strengths that allow you to be good with kids.

I am patient.

I am calm (most of the time).

I think of creative ways to entertain children.

I have good communication skills.

I have lots of energy and enjoy playing games outside with kids.

I can problem-solve and find solutions to disputes.

I am loving and caring (most of the time).

I have lots of energy and stamina (some of the time).

Or you might say, I am good with my hands and can fix things. Expand on that statement to discover other strengths you possess such as:

I have the ability to solve problems.

I am extremely resourceful and self-motivated.

I am physically strong and capable of working with heavy machinery.

I am creative when it comes to fixing things.

I am reliable and trustworthy.

I am currently under construction.
Thank you for your patience.

This is a fun exercise and when you get to the end of your list you will be feeling pretty amazing. When you play to your strengths others will see you as pretty amazing, too.

But as I mentioned we are not all blessed with the same talents and gifts so delegate those things that are not your strengths. You don't have to, nor should you do everything yourself. Allowing others to help you is not a weakness. It is a wise decision as it not only frees up your time to do what you do best, but also reduces stress, because you are not struggling with a task you find difficult.

Armed with your list of strengths try to think how they might be of service to help you achieve your goals and think of new ways you can capitalize on those strengths.

I might wake up early and go jogging,
but I also might win the lottery - The odds are about the same.

When you stack the odds in your favor by playing to your strengths life is easier and anything that makes life easier is amazing.

Life is not a problem to be solved,
but a great adventure.

Be kind to yourself - you are worth it.

Be kind.

Amazing people are kind, not only to others, but also to themselves. They are their own best friend. Think about that for a moment. Are you your own best friend? Do you have your own interests at heart or are you sabotaging your chances of happiness and success and living an amazing life? Do you speak words of encouragement to yourself or criticize every move you make? Do you allow yourself to enjoy life's wins and small victories or do you tell yourself you could have done better?

If the concept of being your own best friend is confusing, allow me to clarify and make a few suggestions.

Take some time for yourself.

Every day carve out some time for yourself and do something that brings you joy. I am very fortunate because I love to create art and write which is also how I earn my living. Perhaps you also derive the same enjoyment from drawing and painting. I realize not everyone is artsy and crafty. Perhaps your "me time" would include listening to or playing a musical instrument. Maybe cultivating a garden gives you pleasure or walking in nature. It really doesn't matter what it is just as long as it is something that gives you pleasure and feeds your soul. Be kind to yourself by giving yourself some "me time" each day.

Give yourself recognition.

It is easy to recognize and acknowledge the achievements of others, but we are often slow to acknowledge our own. That trend has to stop. Take ownership of your past achievements and give yourself the recognition you deserve.

When you do something you're proud of, stop for a minute and dwell on it. Praise yourself and relish the accomplishment. Complement yourself. Pat yourself on the back and say the following: "Kudos to me!"

Be your own cheer leader.

We're all familiar with the inner critic. It's that little voice in our heads that's quick to judge and is always ready with a put-down. Well, it's time for your inner critic to meet your inner advocate.

And who exactly is this inner advocate? It's another voice in your head - the one that defends you. When your inner critic comes at you with ridicule and scorn, your inner advocate jumps in and presents arguments on your behalf. While your inner critic is against you, your inner advocate is for you.

Be kind to yourself by cultivating your inner advocate. (Mine looks like Wwonder Woman and how cool is that? Wonder Woman thinks what I do is awesome)!

Forgive yourself.

We all make mistakes and occasionally mess up.
Perhaps the following statements seem familiar.

You did something in the past that you're not proud of.
You failed to stand up for yourself and are annoyed at yourself for being a pushover.
You know you missed out on a great opportunity because you were too scared to act.
Maybe you failed to follow through on an important goal.
If you're angry at yourself, you need to show yourself kindness - accept that you are only human and you don't always make the right choices in life.
Stop blaming yourself. Resolve to do better from now on and forgive yourself.

When you fail, make a mistake, or do something wrong, you have two choices. You can tear yourself down or you can lift yourself up. People who are kind to themselves choose the latter.

Tell yourself it's going to be OK. Give yourself a morale boost by reminding yourself of your past successes. Then, come up with a plan for dealing with what happened and take action.

Take good care of yourself.

One of the best ways to show yourself kindness is to take good care of yourself. Get enough sleep, eat fruits and vegetables, and get some form of exercise on a regular basis. In addition, choose a way to release stress (drinking wine doesn't count). Be well groomed and take pride in your appearance.

Respect yourself.

Self-respect is valuing yourself for who you are and not allowing others to dictate your value. It's trusting yourself, thinking for yourself, forming your own opinions, and making your own decisions. In addition, it's refusing to compare yourself to others.

I no longer have the energy for meaningless friendships,
forced conversations and unnecessary interactions.
I am logging off.

Allow yourself downtime to decompress.

Did you have a tough day? Did you get into an argument with a co-worker or a friend? Was it one of those days in which everything that could wrong, did go wrong? Be kind to yourself. Try the following:

Soak in a hot tub. Add scented bath oil.

Give yourself a scalp massage. Rub your feet.

Make some hot chocolate with little marshmallows in it and sit back with a good book.

Lock your bedroom door, turn on some music, and dance around in your underwear.

Remind yourself of your good qualities.

Maybe you're a little heavier than "the ideal body type" but you have long lustrous hair. You're not great at sports, but you're an ace at math. Maybe you have a tendency to be melodramatic, but you have a great sense of humor.

How you talk to yourself really matters. Remember the words of Thumper (in Disney's Bambi), "if you can't think of something nice to say, don't say nothing at all." This also applies to how you talk to yourself.

Tell yourself, "I Am Enough."

We've all had times in our lives when we've thought, "I'm not good looking enough, or skinny enough, or smart enough, or strong enough to get what I want." Put a stop to the "I'm not enough" self-talk and replace it with the following:

"I'm enough, just as I am."
"I'm worthy of love and respect."
"I deserve to be happy."
"I deserve to have everything I want."
In addition, tell yourself that nothing has to happen to make you worthy. You are already enough.

It's never too late and you are never too old to master the art of being amazing.

Stop trying to be perfect.

When you set a standard of perfection for yourself you are setting yourself up for failure. After all, perfection is unachievable. Can you think of anything more unkind than making success impossible for yourself?

Honor your dreams.

Don't downplay your dreams by labeling them as silly fantasies. Instead, take your dreams seriously by turning those dreams into goals, and by creating a plan for achieving those goals.

Dream big. There are no limitations to how awesome you can become or how high you can rise except for the limits you put on yourself.

Forget trying to be perfect, instead aim to improve one step at a time.

Show yourself compassion.
Not sure what that looks and feels like? Imagine that someone you love is feeling hurt.

What would you say to them?
How would you treat them?
How would you reassure them?
How would you make them feel cared for and loved?
Now, do that for yourself.

Believe in yourself.
Part of being kind to yourself is wanting the best for yourself and in order to get the best, you have to believe in yourself. Have faith in your own abilities and in your own judgment. I am a daughter first - wife and mother which means I have 3 very important people in my life, whose needs and well being are high on my priority list. You might have a similar list and understand how easy it is to put their needs ahead of your own, but it is also very important not to omit yourself from that list of very important people. You don't have to put yourself at the top of the list but you do have to make sure you are on the list.

I want to remind you of the instructions you receive when traveling on an airplane. "In the event of a decompression, an oxygen mask will automatically appear in front of you. To start the flow of oxygen, pull the mask towards you. Place it firmly over your nose and mouth, secure the elastic band behind your head, and breathe normally. If you are traveling with a child or someone who requires assistance, secure your mask first, and then assist the other person." The airline understands that you need to care for yourself before you can care for someone else.

Get into the habit of living in the moment by practicing mindfulness.
Mindfulness is a way of thinking – focusing on the here and now. It encourages you to pay attention to the present moment. This can help reduce thinking too far ahead (and worrying about things that haven't happened yet), or thinking about the past (and dwelling on things you cannot change). You can mindfully do almost anything – eat a meal, brush your teeth, or choose to go for a walk mindfully.

When I paint and create art work, I am mindful of the colors I choose and how they not only relate to the other colors in the painting, but also how my emotional state at the time influences my choice of color palette.

Try mindfully preparing your next meal. Be aware of the textures, aroma and origin of your ingredients. Be mindful of the transformation that takes place as you mix the ingredients together. Feel gratitude that you have food to eat and a place to prepare it. Think about how the food will taste and how your body will feel as you nourish it with good food.

Life is not always a bed of roses and when we finally make it to the end of a stressful day it's tempting to reward oneself with alcohol or junk food, for example. This kind of treat is OK now and then, but be careful not to use it as a crutch, as it can sabotage all the efforts you've made.

Keep a gratitude journal.
This simple act helps you to notice things in your everyday life that you can be grateful for. These don't have to be huge life changing events. You can be grateful for simple things like having fresh milk to pour on your breakfast cereal. I mentioned earlier that I grew up in the countryside and outhouses were the norm - so I am really grateful for indoor plumbing. People who practice gratitude and notice the things they are thankful for are happier and have a greater sense of wellbeing. You might want to try and think of a few things in the morning or before you go to bed. Maybe you are thankful you woke up without a headache or that you have warm fuzzy slippers to slip your feet into as you get out of bed.

Actively focus on the positives of your day. The more you look for all the reasons you have to be grateful the more you will find and come to realize what an amazing life you have.

Dare to reach into the darkness
to pull someone into the light.
Remember amazing people
not only stand up for themselves,
they stand up for others too.

The Golden Rule.

The Golden Rule is:
Treat others the way you want to be treated. Most people were taught from an early age to treat others with respect and kindness.

If you are wondering how being kind and respectful increases your personal awesomeness think for a moment about the opposite.

If you are witness to someone being rude to a sales clerk in a store, or shouting insults at a driver who is maybe lost and going a little too slow for their liking, or someone treating an animal cruelly I will to go out on a limb here and bet you don't think to yourself "wow that person is amazing."

I am not suggesting we all follow in the footsteps of Mother Theresa who was the epitome of kindness and compassion. What she achieved and the lives she touched made her totally amazing. But following The Golden Rule and treating others the way you would like to be treated has real-life benefits.

Kindness and empathy help us relate to other people and have more positive relationships with friends, family, and even perfect strangers we encounter in our daily lives which is awesome. But exercising your kindness muscle can actually make you healthier.

Kindness releases feel-good hormones. Have you ever noticed that when you do something nice for someone else, it makes you feel better too? This isn't just something that happens randomly—it has to do with the pleasure centers in your brain. Doing nice things for others boosts your serotonin, the neurotransmitter responsible for feelings of satisfaction and well-being. Like exercise, altruism also releases endorphins, a phenomenon known as a "helper's high."

So, go ahead and volunteer, help someone in need,
buy someone coffee or lunch.
It may be just the pick-me-up you need.

Kindness is good for your heart.

Kindness strengthens your heart physically and emotionally. Maybe that's why they say nice, caring people have really big hearts?

Following The Golden Rule is an awesome way to reduces stress.
Finding a solution for the stress created by our over - committed, busy, on-the-go lives may be easier than we think.

Helping others lets you get outside of yourself and your own problems. It allows you to focus on someone else and take a break from the factors or circumstances that are causing stress in your own life. When you step away from your own problems for a little while and boost your feel-good hormones by being kind to someone else, you can very often find a solution that will reduce your own problems.

You should love the Lord your God with all your heart and with all your mind and with all your strength. The second most important commandment is to love your neighbor as yourself. Mark 12:30-31

No such thing as can't.

Have you ever dreamed of achieving some big goal in your life, but have convinced yourself you can't for one or more reasons? You're scared, you're worried you will fail, you're insecure or you just don't know where to start. Or perhaps you pass the buck and place the blame on others he/she wouldn't let me do this or that. Or maybe you use age as an excuse - I am too old or too young. Or I can't afford it. Sometimes lack of sufficient funds may be a valid reason, but remember what my dear old dad told me. "You can have anything you want if you want it badly enough and are willing to do what it takes to get it."

More often than not we give up on our dreams before we have given them a chance to become a reality.

Here are a few ways to help you cope with your day-to-day worries and anxieties about trying something you have never done before.

Breathe through the panic.

Even the thought of trying relatively small (new) things may cause stress and anxiety. If you start to get a faster heartbeat or sweating palms, the best thing is not to fight it. Stay where you are and simply feel the panic without trying to distract yourself. Place the palm of your hand on your stomach and breathe slowly and deeply.

The goal is to help the mind get used to coping with those panicky feelings and realizing it is just a feeling, nothing terrible actually happens and it passes. Recognizing it for what it is helps to make it disappear.

Take time out.

It's impossible to think clearly when you're flooded with fear or anxiety. Distract yourself from the worry for 15 minutes. Try walking around the block, making a cup of herbal tea or taking a soothing bubble bath. I find a walk around the garden pulling a few weeds really helps, plus I clean up the flower beds which is an added bonus.

Face your fears.

Avoiding fears only makes them scarier. Whatever your fear, when you face it, the fear should start to fade. If you panic one day getting into a lift, for example, it's best to get back into a lift the next day.

Imagine the worst.

Try imagining the worst case scenario. Very often the probability of the worst thing actually happening is 1000/1, so you can dismiss it. Or you realize that the worst case scenario isn't really that bad.

If a challenge exists
there must be a solution.

Your amazing life is
found in the space
between your deepest desire
and your greatest fear.

Until you break out of your cage
and spread your wings you will never
know how high you can fly.

Look at the evidence.
Has anyone else done what you would like to do and lived to tell the tale? Odds are they have, but if they did have a fatal accident while attempting what it is you would like to try, perhaps re-think your goals.

Don't try to be perfect.
Life after all is just a human experiment, yet many of us feel that our lives must be perfect. Bad days and setbacks will always happen, and it's important to remember that life is messy.

Talk about it.
Seek out others who have successfully achieved your goal and ask questions. With modern technology and social media this is easier than ever. They will be able to help ease your fears and also give you tips on how to successfully reach your goal.

I am perfect in my imperfections,
secure in my insecurities,
and beautiful in my own way.

Celebrate small victories.
Finally, give yourself a treat. Celebrate each small step towards your goal. Reinforce your success by treating yourself to a massage, a country walk, a meal out, a book, a DVD, or whatever little gift makes you happy.

When faced with
adversity you
have three choices.
You can either
let it define you.
Let it destroy you,
or you can let it
strengthen you .

Linda Finstad

Develop Grit and Gumption

Grit is the second-cousin-twice-removed of Mojo. They have lots of similar family traits. Grit is often referred to as the guy with determination and fortitude to complete any task or goal he sets for himself. He will not waver from the path despite set backs. He has "stick-to-it-ness" if that is a word. Some may call him doggedly stubborn, but this would be meant as a compliment not an insult.

You may have heard of another family member called Gumption.
Gumption is the guy who seems to be dealt hard blows through no fault of his own. As the saying goes. "If he didn't have bad luck he wouldn't have any luck at all." However he manages to summon up the motivation, positivity, hope, enthusiasm, and courage to pick himself up, dust himself off and try again. Amazing people have grit and gumption in spades.

So how do you develop Grit and Gumption in your quest to be amazing?

It is possible to improve your grit and gumption but you will need four things; Purpose, Practice, Hope and Time. This not something you can achieve instantly it will take time to consciously develop this awesome trait.

Purpose

Purpose is a popular buzz word. Self-help gurus and life coaches encourage people to find their true purpose and passion. Only then will they discover their reason for being and be truly happy. I have always found this idea a little high-handed. After all we can be passionate about lots of things and those things can change over time. I am sure the things you were passionate about as a teenager are not the same things you are passionate about as an adult. So let's look at a more down-to-earth definition of purpose and there are a couple that we should consider.

Purpose: The reason for which something is done or created or for which something exists. A toaster was manufactured with the purpose of making toast and the convenience of an easy breakfast. This book was created to entertain, inform and inspire the reader. That was the purpose it was written.

And **Purpose:** A person's sense of resolve or determination. Both the toaster and the book required the resolve and determination of the engineer and author to complete the task.

Your purpose is anything you can develop an interest in over an extended period of time. It isn't some mysterious higher calling or the singular task you were put on this earth to accomplish.

Practice isn't the thing you do once you are good.
It's the thing you do that makes you good.

Practice

This is the definition I found in the dictionary.
Practice: A repeated exercise in or performance of an activity or skill so as to acquire or maintain proficiency in it.

We all know exactly what practice means. After all, we were encouraged to practice our A,B,C's in kindergarten, then as we moved through the years of school we learned and practiced many new skills to round out our education. This means we are all capable of practicing a new skill to become proficient. However, something we need to avoid is repeating the same thing over and over if it is not increasing our skill level, or worse, if it is moving us in the wrong direction. This usually means engaging the help and guidance of someone who has already mastered the skill and is willing to share their expertise and advice.

Einstein once said that insanity is doing the same thing over and over and expecting a different result.

Hope

Not to be confused with optimism, because optimism focuses more broadly on the expected quality of future outcomes in general. Optimism is the belief that things will turn out all right; hope makes no such assumption, but is a conviction that one can act to make things better in some way.

Hope and optimism can go together, but they don't have to. You can be a hopeless optimist who feels personally helpless, but assumes that everything will turn out all right. You can be a hopeful pessimist who makes negative predictions about the future but has confidence that you can improve things in your life and others. Whatever camp you fall into you will agree that failure is often inevitable. No one goes through life without knowing failure of some kind. However, if we learn to embrace failure as an opportunity to learn, improve, and then get back up again, we're more likely to succeed in future attempts. This takes gumption and grit.

To develop more grit you must start with hope and learn that it's alright to fail as long as you don't give up or quit.

Time

The last part of the gumption and grit formula is simply time. It takes time to devote yourself to practice, purpose, and developing from failure. Having something you can be highly interested in, something you can deliberately practice and readily get feedback on, something where you hope that you can succeed, are all important. The key is, of course, giving yourself time to practice and learn and stay in the game.

Success is not achieved instantly but through countless tiny choices. Tim Kennedy

You have been criticizing yourself for years
and it hasn't worked.
Try approving of yourself and see what happens.

Talking to yourself is normal.

Go ahead, talk to yourself.
Talking to yourself isn't just normal, it's also good for your mental health, but only if you have the right conversations.

We talk to ourselves constantly, and one can argue that just thinking things through quietly, without speaking out loud, is the same as talking to ourselves. We talk to ourselves for many reasons. Very often when we're experiencing a heightened emotion, such as anger, nervousness, fear, surprise, or excitement. Sometimes we talk to ourselves when we are trying to figure out a solution for a difficult task or problem or when we are alone and just need someone who really understands us to talk to.

It's OK to talk to yourself - it's even OK to answer yourself.
But when you ask yourself to repeat what you just said
you might have a problem.

When I was first married my husband and I would work side-by-side renovating our fixer -upper home. My hubby was very handy and could fix or repair pretty much anything. He would make comments while he worked. Comments like, "Oh this is not going to work, I can't fix this" or, "I don't have the right tools for this job." They were all very negative comments and to be honest my thoughts were, "Oh no, we will have to hire a professional." It took me a while to realize that he was just talking to himself and did not require me to answer him. If I just left him alone he would figure out what he needed to do to complete the task. I am not even sure he was aware that he was talking out loud.

When we speak out loud, it forces us to slow down our thoughts and process them differently because we engage the language centers of our brain.

What we say to ourselves, when we say it, and how we say it, has a tremendous impact on our self-esteem, beliefs about self-efficacy, and overall sense of worth. This may all seem very obvious, and yet negative self-talk (spoken or thought) still happens regularly. For that reason, it's important to be aware when it happens and to actively nip any negative or derogatory remarks in the bud. Your self- conscious brain is listening and eager to make those statements a reality.

When you misplace your keys and tell yourself, "Oh I am so forgetful and stupid for not remembering where I put them." You are imprinting negative thoughts and beliefs in your brain.

Do not underestimate yourself
by comparing yourself to others.
It's our differences that make us unique
and define just how truly amazing we are.

However you can also use self-talk to your advantage like cheering yourself on before an important event. "You've got this, you are well prepared and it is now your turn to shine." Talking to yourself while making plans for a fun trip with friends or a party, is a great opportunity for self-talk that will boost your mood and self esteem. Seriously "You've got this!"

Think of the popular children's character Bob the Builder. Whenever he was faced with a challenging problem he would say out-loud, "Can we fix it?" Bob's crew would respond, "yes we can." He used positive self-talk to bolster his confidence in his problem solving abilities. Bob the Builder's can-do attitude made him an awesome role model for children. Bob the Builder is exactly the kind of contractor I want to hire for any future home renovations. He is Awesome.

Self-talk can help you work through extreme emotions including anger, sadness, confusion, stress, and frustration. It can help you solve personal problems. Think of it as a verbal journal to yourself.

Talking out loud while studying can help expedite and cement your understanding of the topic. Just as long as you are staying on track and talking about what you are trying to learn.

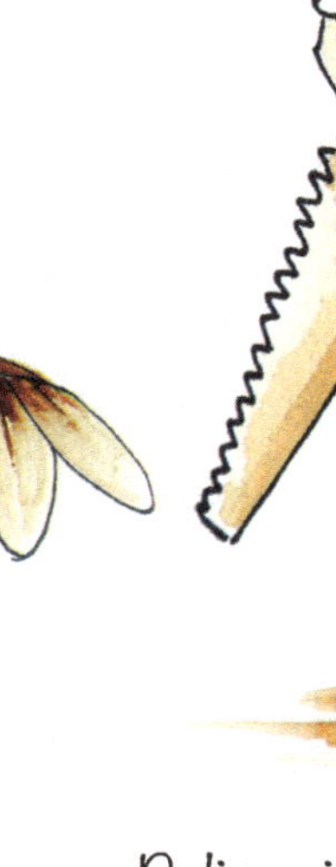

Believe in yourself and you can achieve.

Don't forget to listen. It's important to note that talking to yourself is a two-part process: the talking and the listening. Self-listening, otherwise known as self-awareness, is a primary factor in offering feedback for self-efficacy.

In other words, there's a reason you're feeling compelled to talk out loud, so be sure to also listen to what you're saying, too.

Incidentally, there is no way to talk, to or about cats and come off as a sane person.

Be your own cheerleader.

When you talk to yourself use words of affirmation or words that communicate your love, appreciation, and respect for yourself. Use positive words and phrases and compliments that will encourage and uplift your mood and self-esteem.

If you want to be amazing you really have to believe you are amazing and what better start to the transformation than to tell yourself you are.

Perhaps this sounds a little too much of a stretch. To be honest this only works if you truly believe what you are saying to yourself. Reward yourself by telling yourself that you are amazing for achieving even small victories.

You are amazing - you got up 10 minutes before the alarm went off.
You are amazing - you made a healthy choice for breakfast.
You are amazing - you found matching undies - woo hoo!
You are amazing - you put in a load of washing before leaving for work.
You are amazing - you got to work on time - stress free and feeling good.

These goals are all totally achievable and totally believable which means your brain will believe you are amazing. It seems crazy that we have to try to trick our own brain to believe that we are capable of being amazing, but evidence would suggest that we do.

Self sabotage and why we do it.

You might be feeling a little overwhelmed by the multitude of self-improvement suggestions and I must admit I was a little overwhelmed trying to define and illustrate them. They are all suggestions for implementing change in your actions, thinking and behaviors. As change feels awkward and uncomfortable, we as humans like to avoid things that disrupt our day-to-day patterns, which is why we are all so familiar with the comfort zone. Every life coach worth his salt will tell you that the magic only happens when you step out of your comfort zone. So if we know this, why don't we take that step?

The answer is (forgive me for stating the obvious) because it's uncomfortable. So we procrastinate or find excuses as to why we can't take the step at this moment, perhaps we are too busy. Sometimes we self-sabotage our success to escape uncomfortable feelings. A way to overcome this is to identify your bad habits and actions that prevent you from attaining your goals. In the words of Dr. Phil, "you can't change what you don't acknowledge."

Life will only change when you are
more committed to your dreams
than you are to your comfort zone.

Over the next few days, start to notice your bad habits. Consider the things that suck your time, resources and don't ultimately help you lead an amazing life.

Do you mindlessly scroll through Instagram and Facebook?

That last glass of wine was delicious, but do you then go and open another bottle?

Do you spend hours shopping on-line for things you don't really need?

Do you suffer from impostor syndrome and feel like it is only a matter of time before you are exposed as a fraud?

Is a fear of failing and worrying over perceived outcomes holding you back from stepping out of your comfort zone.

Do you use trips to the fridge for snacks and treats as a way to procrastinate and avoid tackling the task at hand?

These are just a few ways we have devised to self-sabotage our success.

Observe yourself first. Then, start to deliberately do more of the things that make you happy and give you energy. At the same time, work on reducing and then eliminating the habits that squander your time, drain your energy, and ultimately don't make you happy.

Start with small changes and defeat self-sabotage little by little. Allow yourself an allotted amount of time to waste on social media. Get an alarm and when it goes off go and do something else. If you have a glass (or bottle) of wine every day, start by only drinking every other day.
Impostor syndrome is not a real thing - no one is more you than you.
When you catch yourself talking harshly to yourself write it down, then ask yourself, "Is that really true?" Odds are it is greatly exaggerated and not an accurate comment.

The greatest mistake you can make in life is to be continually fearful that you will make one. When trying something new allow yourself to be a beginner. You won't be perfect and proficient the first time you try anything new. When you accept that fact you remove the pressure to be perfect.

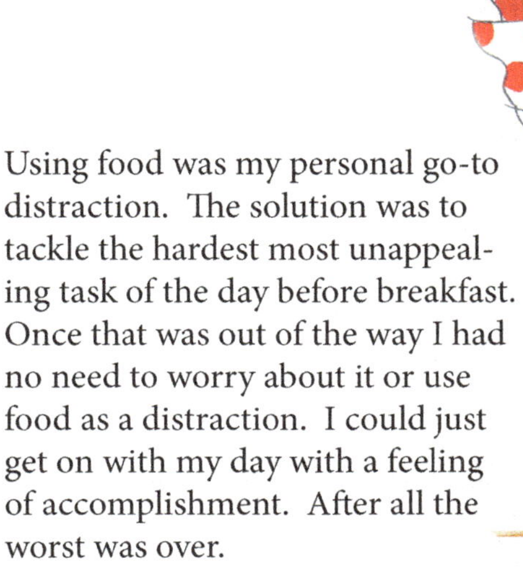

Using food was my personal go-to distraction. The solution was to tackle the hardest most unappealing task of the day before breakfast. Once that was out of the way I had no need to worry about it or use food as a distraction. I could just get on with my day with a feeling of accomplishment. After all the worst was over.

I am glad I don't have to hunt my own food.
I don't even know where chocolate cake lives.

We are not given a good life or a bad life.
We are given a life - it is up to us to make it good or bad.

Focus on what you want.
Overcome the Itty Bitty Shitty Committee.

How much of our lives do we waste focusing on what we don't want instead of embracing what we do want?

Want to know a little secret? One of the most powerful techniques you can use to ensure your immediate and continued success in your quest to be and have an amazing life is to stay focused on what you want. Not just the big finish but all aspects and steps it will take to achieve it.

Nothing new with that piece of advice, but equally important is not to give in to doubt, perceived limitations and current circumstances that might be hampering your progress right now. I know this sounds simple, but most people find it extremely hard to put into practice. You understand the importance of goal setting; you may even have a few goals right now. Your goal may be to earn a certain amount of money or find the courage to ask for a raise. Perhaps you dream of buying your own home, or traveling around the world etc. Sadly after the initial excitement of setting the goal most people settle into their regular routine and nothing changes.

Have you ever attended a motivational seminar or read an inspiring book and been all excited and fired up? You may have taken a few notes and written down some new goals, maybe even taken some action. Then you have been disappointed in your progress or felt seeing any real results was just not fast enough.

I want you to ask yourself:

How much of your thinking is about what you don't want to have happen or about what might happen if something you're trying to accomplish doesn't work out?

The answer to that one question is the key to your ultimate success. You see, the secret to all success is being able to stay focused on exactly what you want regardless of how long it takes, or what else is currently happening, or what temporary obstacles might be in your way. It is this single ability to stay focused, committed and with your eye always trained on the end result you want – no matter what – that will enable you to achieve any goal you can possibly set.

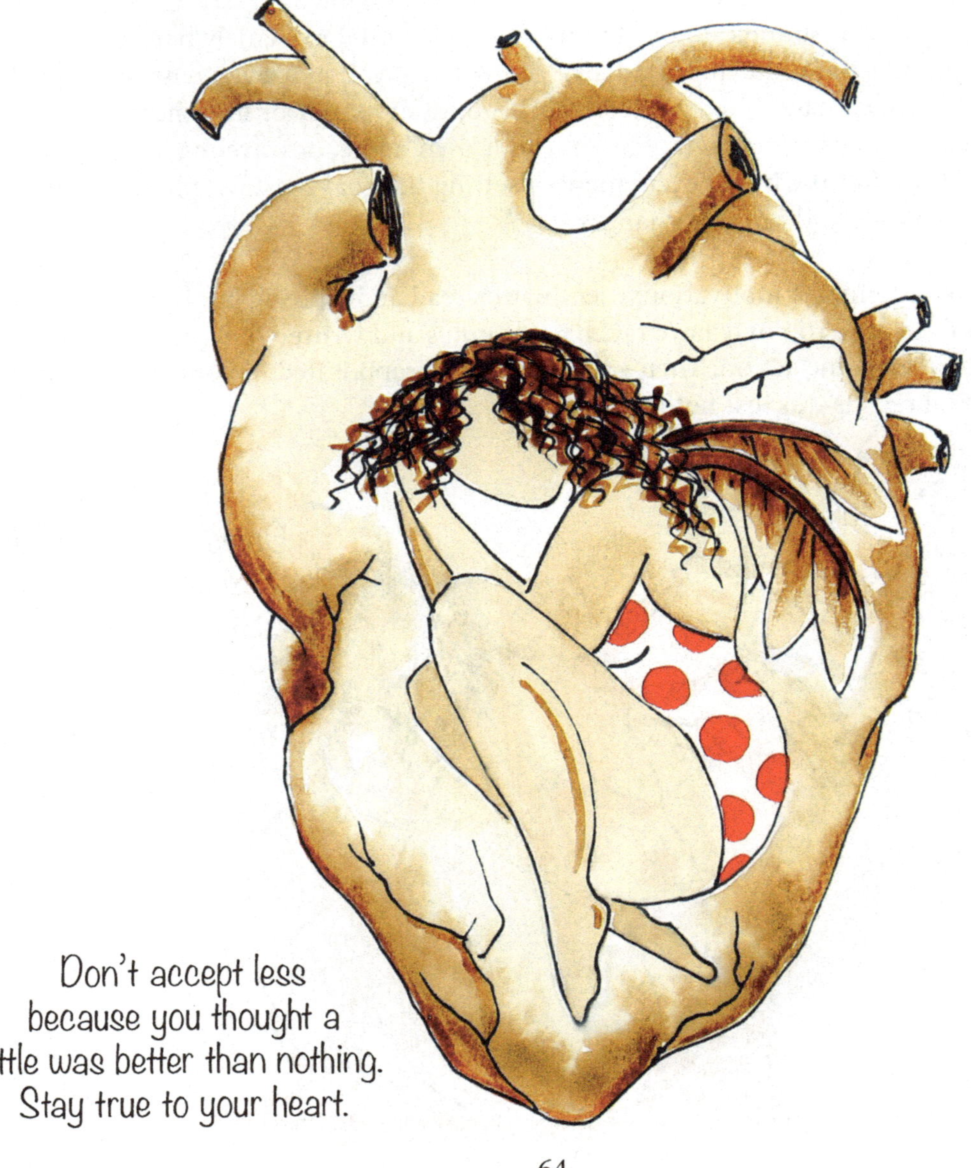

Don't accept less
because you thought a
little was better than nothing.
Stay true to your heart.

So how do you stay focused on what it is you want?
You have to overcome what I affectionately call the Itty Bitty Shitty Committee.
These are the dirty birdies of discontent. That is what I call those negative voices in your head. You know the ones who are quick to point out all the reasons why you can't or shouldn't live life to the fullest. We all have them, even celebrities whose lives (on the outside) look perfect have moments of self doubt. The only difference between us and them is that they have learned how to either shut up the voices or acknowledge them for what they really are, which are unfounded fears and lies. So let's examine a few of those lies the Itty Bitty Shitty Committee like to whisper in your ear to keep you in that safe familiar rut you are trying to escape.

These fictitious worries are not in any particular order. One might resonate with you more than others.

You can't do that!
You never know until you try - if this statement is surrounding something you have never done before there is absolutely no hard evidence to prove that you can't do it. The trick to overcoming this negativity is to treat the new activity as an experiment. Set the parameters, complete the action and examine the results all from a non-personal perspective. If the experiment failed, this was not a personal failure because it was just an experiment and the results merely highlighted where the experiment could be improved.

Don't let anyone tell you
You can't do something.
Just do it!
Proving them wrong is the best
revenge.

Do not be too timid or squeamish
about your actions.
All life is an experiment.

I am too old.

This is one of the worst lies we tell ourselves, and it is not even a real thing. Unlike the line they draw at the entrance to roller coasters that says, "You must be this tall to enter the ride." There is no official age restriction to anything. This age limitation is one we created entirely in our heads and it is different for everyone. One person may think they are too old to go back to school at 35, another may see retirement as the perfect time to engage in further education. The trick to overcoming this hurdle is when you catch yourself thinking, "I am too old to do this or that." Pose the question, "Who made that rule, and where is the evidence to support that?"

Note to self:
You are never too old
and it's never too late
to dream a new dream.

I can't afford that.
I don't have enough money.

OK - sometimes this is true, but only sometimes. If you want something badly enough you will do whatever it takes to gather the funds required to fulfill that dream. Notice I said do whatever it takes, and you have to want it badly enough. I don't believe positive thinking will manifest a bag of money so you can go on a luxury cruise.

I am not pretty enough or skinny enough.

Again I want you to challenge this negative talk by asking, "Who said so?"
Was someone rude enough to actually say those things to you? Try this question, "Do I really care what you think, and who made you the beauty queen judge?"
I know it's easier said than done because as women we all compare ourselves to not just the Photoshopped celebrities on magazine covers but to each other. We compare ourselves to our friends, ladies at church, at social events, even the woman next to you in line at the grocery store. This kind of self-criticism is a total waste of time because, honestly, most people are so worried about what others will think of them they don't really pay that much attention to you.

Coco Chanel said it perfectly,
"I don't care what you think about me. I don't think about you at all."

I don't have the right support.

(We are not talking about bras, although a good-fitting bra is essential for support.)
Do any of these comments sound familiar?
My family and friends think this is a crazy idea and want me to just forget about it.
It would take a team of people to achieve what I want to do and I am just one person.
Perhaps you have a history of chasing rainbows and unicorns and your family groans when you tell them of your latest wild idea. So don't tell them - just do it. This is a strategy I adopted many years ago. It saves a lot of explaining and to be honest they have already made up their minds that my idea is perhaps a little crazy, so I probably won't be able to change their minds.

If you need a team of people to help fulfill your dream start by recruiting just one person, someone who shares your vision and ambition to make this project a reality. Start the project and encourage your friends to help even if it is in a very small way. Not everyone you know will want to commit full-time to your project, however they may be willing to help you for an evening or a couple of hours. Break down areas where you feel you need support in to small bite- sized volunteer opportunities and ask for help.

I don't know where to start.

This statement may sound innocent, but it can be the most crippling of all. Every journey starts with a single step, but if you never take that step you go nowhere.

As a writer this was something I struggled with on a regular basis until I discovered the solution to this mental block. The answer is to forget about starting at the beginning and working systematically through the project. Start in the middle or even at the end or wherever you know two pieces fit together. Think of your project like a jigsaw puzzle - sure it's nice to get all the edges of the puzzle put together first, however occasionally you find a few pieces that just fit and you can work on that area for a little while. When you find another edge piece you can go back to working on the perimeter.

I am working on it.

This is the biggest lie we tell ourselves and it really means this item just gets added from one to-do list to the next, year after year.

For example, I am working on losing that last 10 pounds. How long have you been working on this? If it's longer than 6 months you are not working on it, you are procrastinating.

Stick with people
who pull the magic out of you,
not the madness.

Birds of a feather flock together.

There is a saying that goes, "If you want to soar with the eagles don't hang out with the chickens."

The general gist of this statement is - if you want to be amazing hang out with other amazing people. Avoid the dullards, complainers and those who are stuck in the mud.

Hang out with people who fit your future, not your history.

I remember my mother warning me about kids who were trouble and to be careful who I made friends with. I am sure your mother made similar predictions about running with the wrong crowd. And guess what? She was absolutely right.

Allow me to give you a little back story.
I grew up in the beautiful English countryside and was fortunate enough to have a pony, which meant I made friends with the other kids in the village who also had ponies. We had fun riding out together and competing in the local pony club events. This is probably a very common scenario. Kids who play football probably make friends with other kids on their team. Kids who love to read and hang out in the library tend to gravitate to other kids who love to read.

Spending time with people who are just like you is easy and feels comfortable. You have lots in common and friendships are easily formed. However, to raise your level of awesomeness you need to hang out with awesome people. Awesome people see things and opportunities we may otherwise not be aware of. They think differently than us and tend to have more life experiences. The good news is that you can absorb some of their awesomeness by osmosis, just by hanging out with them.

Even if you only absorb 10% of their awesomeness - little by little you will raise your game.

When you hang out with amazing people, you will learn new things. People who have more knowledge and experience than you can help expose you to many new concepts and ideas. Having people of excellent and exceptional talents and skills in your circle has many benefits. You learn much more from those you spend time with whilst enjoying their company.

So where do you find these awesome people ?

Awesomeness by osmosis

When I made the decision to become a full-time artist I joined several art clubs and associations. Many of these clubs offered workshops and classes which I eagerly signed up for. They also had drop-in painting sessions where members could come to the club and paint together. This was the perfect setting to make friends and learn from the other club members. I always made sure I set up my easel close to the more talented and serious artists in the club so I could chat and ask questions about both art and the pros and cons of being a full-time artist. They were flattered by my attention and because we shared similar interests it was easy to make friends.

Amazing people have the ability to view and analyze things from various points of view. Discussions and conversations will lead you to develop a more open view to new ideas, increasing your adaptability, and embracing new thoughts.

When you spend time with amazing people you will feel inspired and motivated to find true happiness. They have a zest for life which is irresistible and sparks a desire to have that in your own life. It is essential to spend time with motivated and enthusiastic people because their enthusiasm for life is contagious and encourages you to accomplish things you maybe thought you were unable to.

Amazing people give better advice.
If you are struggling with a problem or situation it is crucial that you seek smart, intelligent, worldly-wise people to ask. When you are surrounded by people who are wiser and more knowledgeable than you, your journey will be so much easier. Smart people help you make smart decisions. The opposite is also true, so choose your friends wisely.

Amazing people are not arrogant.
Some people choose to hang out with those who are less intelligent, productive and successful than they are. Because they want to stay at the top of the pack this is purely for egotistical reasons and serves to satisfy their arrogance. These people are not going anywhere in life because they believe they are already at the top. To increase your awesomeness It is essential to spend time with those who have more knowledge or success than you. This means that you already have taken a step to defeat the so-called arrogance. You will be become a better and more humble person as a result and humility is a wonderful trait that will open more doors and gain more respect than promoting yourself as the best.

Osmosis in action.

When you spend time with more successful people, you will also develop an urge to achieve those levels of success. You will also learn from their experiences and stories of how they achieved this success in their lives. They will motivate you, and you will start feeling the change in your attitude. This positive change is possible only when you choose your company carefully. Hang out with people you think can help to increase your knowledge, positivity and awesomeness.

If you are lucky enough to become friends with amazing people they can help you to see your personality in a brighter light. They will shed light on the things which are in need of improvement. Their comments and opinions can help you a lot developing your personality to achieve success.

Never give up on your goal to be amazing
because of the time it will take.
The time will pass anyway.

Be more and more amazing every day.

"It is never too late to be who you might have been." George Eliot

I hope you are inspired to make a few easy changes that will make your life more amazing. Although there are lots of suggestions in this book, you don't need to do them all at once. If you make small incremental changes every day you will become a little bit more confident, a little bit more adventurous, a little bit more relaxed and happy, a bit more patient, and on and on.

If you aim for just 1% improvement every day, all those small improvements will add up to something significant. Taking big leaps in order to accomplish the goal in as little time as possible may sound good in theory, but often ends in burnout, frustration, and failure. Instead, we should focus on continuous improvement by slowly and slightly adjusting our normal everyday habits and behaviors.

Do not be fooled into thinking that change is only meaningful if there is some large, visible outcome associated with it, whether it is losing weight, building a business, traveling the world or any other goal. There is a tendency to believe that we need to make some earth-shattering improvement that everyone will talk about for those changes to have any value. But that is not true!

Improving by just 1% isn't noteworthy (sometimes it isn't even noticeable). When you start this process, there is basically no difference between making a choice that is 1% better or 1% worse. Neither one will impact you very much today. As time goes on, these small improvements or declines compound and you suddenly find a very big gap between people who make slightly better decisions on a daily basis and those who don't.

If you get 1% better each day for one year, you'll end up thirty-seven times better by the time you're done. I am not really sure of the math, but you will definitely be more amazing.

Here are a few tips on how you can incrementally improve your awesomeness factor.

Do more of what already works.

Don't ignore your existing resources, ideas and possibilities because they don't seem new and exciting. Here are just a few examples of small changes that, have the capacity to drive progress and improve our lives, especially if we just do them with more consistency.

Floss every day.

Never miss workouts.

Just do the awkward and uncomfortable tasks at the start of the day rather than procrastinating.

Be kind to yourself and others.

Send more thank you and greeting cards.

Be quick to apologize when you are in the wrong.

Eat your greens and beans.

The trick to making this strategy work for you is to document your successes and failures and learn from both experiences.

Progress often hides behind boring solutions and unnoticed insights. You really don't need yet another self-help book or a life coach. You just need to do more of what already works.

Avoid tiny losses.

In many cases, improving your awesomeness factor is not about doing more things right, but about doing fewer things wrong. This idea is called improvement by subtraction, which encourages you to recognize and do less of what doesn't work. Strip away the inessential and make-work projects (busyness for the sake of being busy) and free up your time to focus on being awesome.

Einstein said, "The definition of insanity is doing the same thing over and over and expecting a different result."

Or if you prefer a modern day advisor - in the words of Dr. Phil "You can't change what you don't acknowledge."

The easiest way to identify what you need to stop doing is to write down the steps leading up to things that went wrong. I don't need to explain how these common mistakes came about and how easy it would have been to make small changes in your actions to avoid them.

You ran out of gas half way to work.
You lost money at the casino.
You had a hangover.
You felt sick after eating a whole tub of icecream.
You feet had blisters caused by your new high heel shoes.
You missed your flight (so also missed a day of your holiday).
The dress you had been saving for a special occasion doesn't fit anymore.

In reality, it is often easier to improve your performance by cutting out actions that create a downside rather than thinking of new actions that would create an upside. Subtraction in the game of life is often easier than addition.

Don't let the sadness of your past
and the fear of your future
ruin the happiness of your present.

Measure your progress by looking backward.
We often measure our progress by looking forward. We set goals. We plan milestones for our progress. Basically, we try to predict the future to some degree. Measuring backward means you acknowledge your progress and see how far you have come. This gives you incentive to carry on your journey to living a happy and amazing life by making choices and decisions based on what has already happened, not on what you want to happen.

As you make better and better choices your life will get better and better which means you have mastered the art of being Amazing.

Be like the Bee
Sip life's sweet moments
Mind your own beezwax
Create a buzz
and always find your way home.

I hope you enjoyed my tips and life hacks to living a happy and amazing life and were inspired by the everyday coffee angels I used to illustrate some of the more important points. This is typically where the author would print in bold letters

The End.

But of course, this is just the beginning.

Get ready for a new chapter - in your new life.

Bonus Chapter

10 easy life hacks to happiness.

For those who are too busy to read the entire book.

1. Stop Stuffing your life with stuff.

One of the biggest things we need to do to be happier is to let go of the desire for more stuff. Living in a consumer-driven society, we're endlessly sold the notion that happiness lies with a new car, a youth-defying serum, or dream holiday that we simply must have.

You can't buy happiness and studies consistently show that when people reflect on their happiest moments, those are events (like a child's first steps), not a new handbag or wide-screen TV.

When I get tired of walking around the mall
I sit down and try on shoes.

2. Say bye-bye to busyness.

Busyness has got a grip on us to the point that we're not enjoying the richness of life, we're just skimming the surface of it. This epidemic of busyness is a huge impediment to happiness. Don't wear it like a badge of honor. You have the power to put the brakes on and re-evaluate what must stay and what should go from your to-do list.

Your worth is not measured by your productivity.

3. Accept that you can't control events – only your reactions to them.

It's a misconception that it's bad drivers, traffic jams or computer viruses that make you angry. You decide to be angry when you react to them. It's a choice and, hard as it may be, you can choose to react differently. If you change your internal world, your external world changes, or at least your experience of the external world will change.

Don't be controlled by circumstance.
Live your life on your own terms.

4. Steer clear of vendettas.

This happens when you magnify tiny irritations into full-blown hate campaigns. Acknowledge them for what they really are and choose to let them go. You will ultimately be much happier.

Grudges are a perfect waste of happiness.
Laugh when you can, apologize when you should
and let go of what you can't change.

5. Beware Negativity.

It's very easy to fall into the trap of being a bit of a moaner, but constantly wallowing in boredom, sameness, drizzle and tiredness can become habitual. Whining and complaining doesn't do you any good nor does it make you fun to be around, so do everyone a favor and get out of the negativity rut.

Happy people find a way to live with their problems, and miserable people let their problems stop them from living.

6. Smile!

Most people smile when they are happy, but it's actually a two-way street. We smile because we're happy, and smiling causes the brain to release dopamine, which makes us even happier. That doesn't mean you have to go around with a fake smile plastered on your face all the time, but the next time you find yourself feeling low, crack a smile and see what happens. If that feels too forced, head over to Youtube where there are oodles of really funny videos that are guaranteed to put a smile on your face.

Let us always meet each other with a smile
for a smile is the beginning of love.

7. Be grateful.

Simply being grateful can give your mood a big boost. Start each day by acknowledging one thing you're grateful for. You can do this while you're brushing your teeth or just waiting for that snoozed alarm to go off. As you go about your day, try to keep an eye out for pleasant things in your life. They can be big things, such as knowing that someone loves you or getting a well-deserved promotion. They can also be little things, such a cup of coffee with a splash of Baileys or the neighbor who waved to you. Maybe even just the warmth of the sun on your skin.

You don't always need a plan.
Sometimes you just need to breathe, trust, let go
and see what happens.

8. Eat with mood in mind.

You already know that food choices have an impact on your overall physical health, but some foods can also affect your state of mind.

Carbohydrates release serotonin, a "feel good" hormone. Just keep simple carbs and foods high in sugar and starch to a minimum. That sugar rush, energy surge is short-lived and you'll crash.

Complex carbs such as vegetables, beans, and whole grains are a better choice.

Lean meat, poultry, legumes, and dairy are high in protein. These foods release dopamine and norepinephrine, which boost energy and concentration.

Highly processed or deep-fried foods tend to leave you feeling down and so will skipping meals. Start by making one better food choice each day.

For example, swap a big, sweet breakfast pastry for some Greek yogurt with fruit. You'll still satisfy your sweet tooth, and the protein will help you avoid a mid-morning energy crash.

The secret to happiness is great food and great company.

9. Exercise.

There are hundreds of books and videos all touting the virtues of regular exercise and its benefits. But in short, getting physical can help to reduce stress, feelings of anxiety, and symptoms of depression while boosting self-esteem and happiness. Even a small amount of physical activity can make a difference. You don't have to train for a triathlon or climb a mountain to feel the benefits. Unless, that's what makes you happy, of course.

Exercise - your future self will thank you for this.

10. You only need four minutes to be Amazing.

It takes around four minutes for other people to 'catch' your vibe. So if you are upbeat, passionate and positive for four minutes, the people around you will have almost no choice but to feel good, too. Really, who can't slap a smile on their face and fake it for a mere four minutes? The positive feedback from those around you and the endorphins it generates in you will make you want to do it again.

Stay committed to your goals
but flexible in your approach.

More Books
Written
and
illustrated
(with coffee art)
by Linda Finstad.

Available on Amazon

Linda Finstad has created an extensive body of artwork arranged in several collections and published 26 books, both fiction and nonfiction.

This collection is centered around her deep love for horses.

The Horse Watcher
How to De-Code Equine Body Language
The Humans of Horse Racing
How to Photograph Horses and their Humans
How to put Butts in Seats n Saddles
Don't Shoot the Horses
Don't Shoot the Trainer

This series combines Linda's fine art photography with inspiring Bible verses.

Bible Verses for Horse Lovers
How to Identify your Spirit Horse
Bible Verses for Cowboy's
Bible Verses for Horse Crazy Kids
The Cowboys Trail to Salvation

Linda wrote and illustrated 2 delightful children's books.

Shortie the Shetland Pony
Katy Goes to Camp

Last, but not least, there are 2 hilarious (adult humor) books.
These depict a light hearted look at life through the eyes of a chicken.

Chicken Wisdom
More Chicken Wisdom

All titles by Linda Finstad are available on Amazon.

Who is Linda Finstad?

Artist, author, fine art photographer and all-round good egg are just a few words commonly used to characterize Linda Finstad. However, those who know her better would lovingly describe her as an eccentric old bat. This portrayal more accurately describes her quirky personality and extraordinary way of not only looking at life, but also capturing it in her creative endeavors. Chicken Wisdom is a perfect example of her unique perspective, wicked sense of humor and colorful art work.

Why coffee and why angels?

Stuck at home, during the pandemic Linda decided to get creative with what she could find in her kitchen and began painting with coffee. What started out as a little experiment quickly transformed her art practice. Her everyday angels with their generous curves and big attitudes became a huge hit. Her fans and followers were requesting these sassy angels as prints, greeting cards and, of course the books have been extremely popular. To date Linda has created over 800 coffee paintings and is still inspired to create more. You can see the full collection of her coffee art at:

www.FamousCoffeeArtist.com

Lest we forget
Poppy collection

Simply Human collection

3D sculpted Florals

Contemporary Landscapes

Art collections by Linda Finstad

See more art by Linda Finstad at www.FamousCoffeeArtist.com

Made in the USA
Columbia, SC
13 June 2022

61699360R00057

MW01634998

Lübeck

Sachbuchverlag Karin Mader

Fotos und Text:
Uwe Bremse
Foto Seite 11: Martin Mader

Grasberg 1997

Übersetzungen:
Englisch: Michael Meadows
Französisch: Mireille Patel

Printed in Germany

ISBN 3-921957-25-7

In dieser Serie sind erschienen:

Aschaffenburg
Baden-Baden
Bad Oeynhausen
Bad Pyrmont
Bochum
Bonn
Braunschweig
Bremen
Bremerhaven
Buxtehude
Celle
Cuxhaven
Darmstadt
Darmstadt und der Jugendstil
Duisburg
Die Eifel
Eisenach
Erfurt
Essen
Flensburg
Freiburg
Fulda
Gießen
Göttingen
Hagen
Hamburg
Der Harz
Heidelberg
Herrenhäuser Gärten
Hildesheim
Kaiserslautern
Karlsruhe
Kassel
Kiel
Koblenz
Krefeld
Das Lipperland
Lübeck
Lüneburg
Mainz
Mannheim
Marburg
Die Küste – Mecklenburg-Vorpommern
Minden
Mönchengladbach
Münster
Das Neckartal
Oldenburg
Osnabrück
Die Küste – Ostfriesland
Paderborn
Recklinghausen
Der Rheingau
Rostock
Rügen
Die Küste – Schleswig-Holstein Nordsee
Die Küste – Schleswig-Holstein Ostsee
Schwerin
Siegen
Stade
Sylt
Trier
Tübingen
Ulm
Wiesbaden
Wilhelmshaven
Wolfsburg
Würzburg
Wuppertal

Titelbild:
An der Untertrave zwischen der Meng- und Holstenstraße

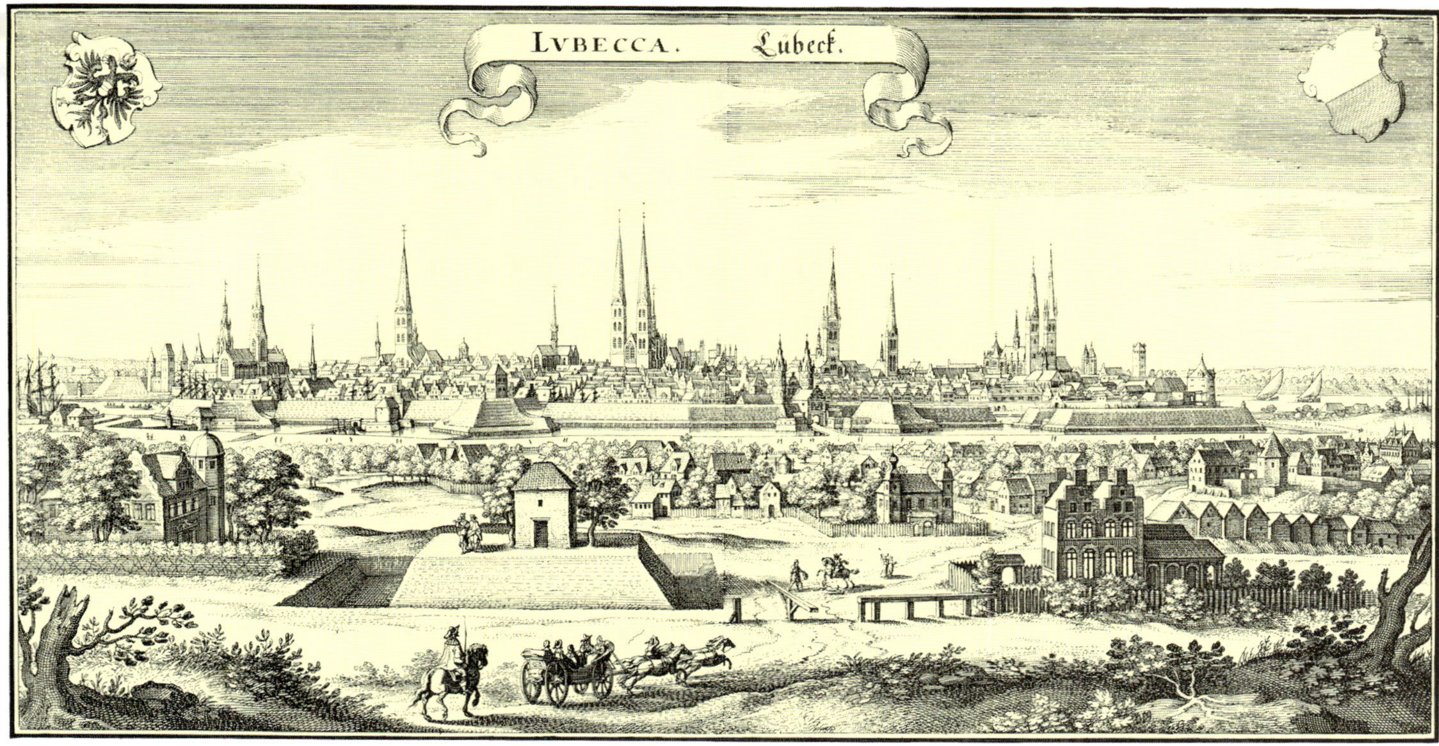

Lübeck aus: Matthäus Merian "Topographia Germaniae", 1653

Die Hansestadt Lübeck entwickelte sich im Mittelalter zur Königin der Hanse und Perle der Backsteingotik. Die in dieser Zeit entstandenen Gebäude wurden Vorbild für viele Bauten im gesamten Ostseeraum.
Heute zeigt sich die Großstadt als Einkaufs- und Kongreßzentrum, als Universitätsstadt, und als größter Fährhafen Europas mit einer Brückenfunktion nach Skandinavien.
Im Jahre 1987 erhielt Lübeck die Anerkennung als Weltkulturerbe durch die UNESCO, weil die Stadt eine gut erhaltene mittelalterliche Stadtanlage hat.

The Hanseatic city of Lübeck developed into the queen of the Hanseatic League and a gem of Gothic brickwork architecture during the Middle Ages. The buildings constructed during this time became models for many edifices in the entire Baltic Sea region.
Today the big city displays itself as a shopping and convention center, a university town and as Europe's largest ferry port with its "bridge" to Scandinavia.
In 1987 Lübeck received recognition for its international cultural heritage by UNESCO because the city possesses a well preserved medieval Old Town.

La ville hanséatique de Lübeck était au Moyen Age la reine de la Hanse et la perle du gothique de brique. Les bâtiments qui furent élevés à cette époque servirent de modèle architectural dans tous les pays de la Baltique.
De nos jours, c'est une grande ville, un centre d'achats et de congrès et une ville universitaire. C'est le plus grand port de ferry d'Europe et il sert de pont avec la Scandinavie.
Les constructions médiévales bien conservées de la ville lui valurent d'être reconnue héritage culturel mondial par l'UNESCO en 1987.

Ein Rundgang durch die historische Altstadt

Einen Stadtrundgang durch die historische Altstadt von Lübeck beginnt man am besten am Holstentor. „Concordia domi foris pax" – Eintracht innen, außen Friede – kündet in großen Buchstaben der Wahlspruch der Lübecker. Von der Aussichtsplattform der Petrikirche hat man eine eindrucksvolle Sicht über die alte Hansestadt und besonders über den Stadtteil St. Lorenz.

The best place to begin a tour through the historical Old Town of Lübeck is at Holstentor. "Concordia domi foris pax" – harmony within, peace without – is proclaimed in large letters as the motto of the people of Lübeck. From the observation platform of the Petri Church one has an impressive view over the old Hanseatic city, especially over the district of St. Lorenz.

Qui veut visiter la vieille ville historique de Lübeck commencera, de préférence, à la Holstentor. «Concordia domi foris pax» – concorde à l'intérieur, paix à l'extérieur – annonce en grosses lettres la devise des habitants de Lübeck. Du haut de la Petrikirche l'on a une vue impressionnante sur la vieille ville hanséatique et, en particulier, sur le quartier de St. Lorenz.

Neben dem Holstentor befinden sich sechs Salzspeicher aus dem 16. bis 18. Jahrhundert. Anfangs dienten diese Gebäude als Heringshäuser, später wurde hier wirklich Salz gespeichert, das aus Lüneburg kam. Hinter den Salzspeichern auf der Trave konnten die Schiffe bis an die Gebäude heranfahren.

Next to Holstentor there are six salt storehouses dating from the 16th to 18th century. At first these buildings served as herring houses, later salt from Lüneburg was really stored here. Behind the salt storehouses ships were able to sail on the Trave right up to the buildings.

A côté de la Holstentor se trouvent six entrepôts à sel des 16, 17 et 18e siècles. Ces bâtiments servaient, tout d'abord, à emmagasiner les harengs. Plus tard, l'on entreposa ici le sel venant de Lüneburg. Sur la Trave, à l'arrière, les bâteaux pouvaient parvenir jusqu'aux bâtiments.

An der Obertrave zeigt sich nach Westen eine interessante Abfolge von Hausgiebeln. Der an der Architektur interessierte Besucher wird die abwechslungsreiche Gestaltung der geschlossenen Bauweise bewundern. Immer wieder wird der Blick von den großartigen Hausfassaden gefangengenommen.

An interesting sequence of house gables displays itself towards the west on the Upper Trave. Visitors interested in architecture will admire the varied design of the unified style of construction. One's view is captured again and again by the magnificent facades.

Au bord de l'Obertrave, vers l'ouest, se trouve une succession remarquable de pignons. Le visiteur qui s'intéresse à l'architecture admirera la variété de conception de cet ensemble de bâtiments. On ne peut détacher le regard de ces admirables façades.

Der Bäckergang ist eine Verbindung zwischen der Fischergrube und der Engelsgrube. Es ist ein typischer Altstadtgang, der in den letzten Jahren saniert worden ist. Dadurch ist er ein beliebter Wohngang geworden. Besonders stilvoll ist das Fachwerkhaus mit seinem Reihenhauscharakter.

Bäckergang is a connection between Fischergrube and Engelsgrube. It is a typical Old Town passageway that has been renovated in recent years. It has thus become popular for walks through this pedestrian-only section. The half-timbered house with its row house character is particularly stylish.

Le Bäckergang réunit la Fischergrube à l'Engelsgrube. Ce passage qui a été assaini ces dernières années, est typique d'une ville ancienne. C'est pourquoi il est devenu un lieu résidentiel très apprécié. La maison à colombage a un cachet très particulier.

In der Großen Petersgrube kann ein Ensemble alter Hausgiebel bestaunt werden. Die Baustile der Gotik, des Barocks, des Rokkokos und der Klassizistik wechseln sich hier ab. In mehreren Häusern ist heute die Musikhochschule Lübeck würdevoll untergebracht.

In Große Petersgrube an ensemble of old gables can be admired. The architectural styles of the gothic, baroque, rococo and classicist periods alternate here. Today the Lübeck College of Music has a dignified location in several houses.

Dans la Große Petersgrube on peut admirer un ensemble de vieux pignons où alternent les styles gothique, baroque, rococo et néo-classique. Plusieurs de ces admirables locaux abritent l'Ecole Supérieure de Musique de Lübeck.

Unterhalb der Petrikirche hat sich Ecke Kolk/St. Jürgen Gang ein interessantes Puppentheater mit über 1000 Puppen aus aller Welt etabliert. In der Nähe gibt es auch ein Marionettentheater, das groß und klein mit seinen Aufführungen begeistert.

Below the Petrikirche an interesting doll and puppet theater with over 1000 dolls and puppets from all over the world has established itself in Kolk/St. Jürgen Gang. Nearby there is also a marionette theater whose performances entertain both young and old.

Près de la Petrikirche, dans Kolk/St. Jürgen Gang, se trouve un musée intéressant. Il présente plus de 1000 poupées venant du monde entier. Dans le voisinage il y a aussi un théâtre de marionettes dont les représentations remplissent d'enthousiasme petits et grands.

An der Untertrave liegen seit einigen Jahren mehrere Oldtimer-Schiffe. Hier weht ein Hauch von Gemütlichkeit; und von Jahr zu Jahr nimmt die Anzahl der Schiffe „aus der guten alten Zeit" zu. Außerdem wird man durch die alten Schiffe immer wieder daran erinnert, daß Lübeck schon im Mittelalter ein bedeutender Ostseehafen war.

Several old-timer ships have been kept on the Lower Trave for some years. There is an atmosphere of old-fashioned cosiness here; and from year to year the number of ships "from the good old days" increases. Moreover, one is reminded again and again by these old ships that Lübeck was already a significant Baltic Sea port during the Middle Ages.

Dans la Untertrave sont ancrés, depuis quelques années, quelques vieux navires. Ici l'on respire un air du bon vieux temps. Les bateaux deviennent plus nombreux d'année en année et rappellent que Lübeck était, dès le Moyen Age, un port important sur la Baltique.

Das Lübecker Rathaus entwickelte sich am Marktplatz aus ehemaligen Gewandhäusern seit den Jahren 1230/40. Im Jahre 1235 wurde die gotische Schaufassade mit den beiden Windlöchern errichtet; und in der zweiten Hälfte des 16. Jahrhunderts entstand die Sandstein-Laube im Stil der Renaissance. Die in der Palmsonntagnacht 1942 zerstörte ehemalige Kriegsstube (rechts) zeigt ihren gotischen Schmuck mit Türmchen, Windlöchern und Wappenschildern. Das Lübecker Rathaus wurde im Mittelalter zum Vorbild für weitere Rathäuser im Ostseeraum.

Lübeck's Town Hall developed out of former cloth merchant houses at the marketplace beginning in the years 1230/40. In 1235 the Gothic ornamental facade was built with the two openings; and in the second half of the 16th century the sandstone pergola was constructed in Renaissance style. The former war conference room (on right), which was destroyed during Palm Sunday night in 1942, displays its Gothic ornamentation with little towers, openings and shields with coats-of-arms. During the Middle Ages Lübeck's Town Hall became a model for other town halls in the Baltic Sea region.

Des constructions pour les drapiers sont à l'origine de l'hôtel de ville que l'on commença à construire à partir de 1230/40. En 1235 fut élevée la façade gothique avec ses deux soupiraux. Les arcades de grès, de style Renaissance, datent de la deuxième moitié du 16e siècle. L'ancienne Kriegsstube (à droite), détruite le dimanche des Rameaux 1942, est ornementée de tourelles, de soupiraux et de blasons gothiques. Au Moyen Age, l'hôtel de ville de Lübeck devint un modèle pour d'autres hôtels de ville dans les pays baltiques.

Das Schabbelhaus in der Mengstraße 48 hat eine alte Restaurant-Tradition und gehört zu den führenden Häusern seiner Branche. Im Saal erkennt man an den hochgezogenen Fenstern das alte Lübecker Dielenhaus. Durch die bis zu fünf Meter hohen Fenster sollte mehr Licht in die Diele fallen.

Schabbelhaus at Mengstraße 48 has an old restaurant tradition and is among the leading establishments in its trade. One recognizes the old Lübeck hall-type house in the high windows. More light was supposed to come into the large hall through windows that are up to five meters in height.

Au no 48 de la Mengstraße, la Schabbelhaus, un restaurant dont la tradition est fort ancienne, est l'un des principaux établissements de cette branche. On reconnaît les hautes fenêtres de l'ancienne «Dielenhaus» typique des maisons de Lübeck. La lumière entrait dans le vestibule (Diele) par des fenêtres qui pouvaient avoir jusqu'à cinq mètres de haut.

Das Buddenbrookhaus in der Mengstraße 4 stammt von 1758. Erhalten blieb allerdings nur die Barockfassade mit dem Figurenschmuck von D.J. Boy, der auch die Figuren der Puppenbrücke geschaffen hat. Dieses Haus, durch Thomas Manns Roman „Die Buddenbrooks" berühmt geworden, ist aber nicht sein Geburtshaus.

Buddenbrookhaus at Mengstraße 4 dates from 1758. But only the baroque facade with the decorative figures by D.J. Boy, who also created the figures of the Puppet Bridge, remained intact. This house, which became famous by virtue of Thomas Mann's novel "Die Buddenbrooks", is not his house of birth, however.

La maison Buddenbrook, au no 4 de la Mengstraße, date de 1758. Seule la façade baroque, décorée de personnages, a été conservée. Elle est l'œuvre de D.J. Boy qui exécuta aussi les statues du pont «Puppenbrücke». Cette maison, rendue célèbre par le roman de Thomas Mann «Die Buddenbrooks», n'est pas la maison natale de cet homme de lettres.

Uhren
Peschlow
Peschlow

Die Breite Straße mit der eintürmigen Jakobikirche ist als Fußgängerzone die Einkaufsstraße Lübecks.
Das Kanzleigebäude (Bild rechts) schließt sich in der Breite Straße an das Rathaus nach Norden an, benachbart zur Marienkirche. Das Gebäude reicht seit 1614 bis zur Mengstraße. Die Fassade von 1791 zeigt Hausteineinlagen aus Kalksandstein, die die Backsteinarchitektur beleben. In diesem Gebäude war die Schreibstube des Rates untergebracht.

Breite Straße, with the single-tower Jakobi Church, is a pedestrian zone and Lübeck's shopping street.
The Kanzleigebäude (picture on right) adjoins the Town Hall to the north on Breite Straße, adjacent to Marienkirche. The building has extended to Mengstraße since 1614. The facade dating from 1791 displays ashlar inlay stone work made of sand-lime brick that animates the brickwork architecture. The writing room of the town council was located in this building.

La Breite Straße, où se trouve la Jakobikirche à une tour, est une voie piétonne et la rue commerçante de Lübeck.
Le Kanzleigebäude (à droite), voisin de la Marienkirche, est contigu, vers le nord, à l'hôtel de ville. Depuis 1614, cet édifice s'étend jusqu'à la Mengstraße. Dans la façade de 1791 sont insérées des pierres de grès qui enjolivent l'architecture de brique. Ce bâtiment abritait la chancellerie du conseil municipal.

Neben St. Jakobi befindet sich die Schiffergesellschaft, das Haus der Schiffer, mit einer interessanten Innenausstattung. Das Treppengiebelhaus wurde im Jahre 1535 errichtet. Auf den beiden Beischlagwangen vor dem Portal steht der Spruch „Allen zu gefallen …“ (links) „… ist unmöglich“ (rechts).

The Sailors' Association, the House for Sailors, with its interesting interior furnishings is located next to St. Jakobi. The stepped gable house was built in 1535. On the two sides of the entrance in front of the portal is the saying “Pleasing everyone …” (on the left) “… is impossible” (on the right).

A côté de St. Jakobi se trouve la Maison de la Corporation des Marins (Haus der Schiffer) dont la décoration intérieure et le mobilier sont remarquables. Cette maison avec un pignon en escalier fut construite en 1535. Sur les deux panneaux devant le portail, est inscrite la maxime: «Plaire à tous» (à gauche) «est impossibile» (à droite).

Langjährige intensive Bemühungen Lübecker Musikfreunde führten zum Bau der Musik- und Kongreßhalle, der Lübecker MUK, auf der Wallhalbinsel. Seit dem 1. 10. 1994 finden hier neben national und international bedeutsamen Konzerten, Musical- und Theateraufführungen, auch Kongresse, Ausstellungen und Messen in der in einer Schiffsform gebauten MUK an der Trave statt.

Many years of intensive efforts on the part of music lovers in Lübeck led to the building of the Music and Convention Hall, the so-called Lübeck MUK, on the Wall peninsula. In addition to concerts of national and international renown, musical and theater performances as well as conventions, exhibitions and fairs have been taking place in this complex on the Trave, designed in the shape of a ship, since October 1, 1994.

Grâce aux efforts longs et intenses d'habitants de Lübeck, amis de la musique, le Palais de la Musique et des Congrès (le MUK) a pû voir le jour sur la péninsule de «Wall». Depuis le 1er octobre 1994, des concerts d'envergure tant nationale qu'internationale, des comédies musicales et pièces de théâtre, mais également des congrès, expositions et salons ont lieu dans le MUK, ce bâtiment prenant la forme d'un bateau et se dressant sur les berges de la Trave.

Die Stiftungshöfe sind Gründungen wohlhabender Lübecker zugunsten der Armen. Der Haasenhof (Bild oben) von Magdalena Haase aus dem Jahre 1727 ist die jüngste Einrichtung dieser Art mit einem sehr dekorativen Vorsteherzimmer. Der Füchtings Hof (Bild rechts) von Johann Füchting ist der geräumigste.

The foundation courtyard edifices were set up for the benefit of the poor by wealthy Lübeck citizens. Haasenhof (picture above) of Magdalena Haase, dating from 1727, is the newest facility of this kind with a very decorative chairman's room. Füchtings Hof (picture on right) of Johann Füchting is the most spacious.

Les «Stiftungshöfe» sont des établissements fondés par les riches bourgeois de Lübeck pour les pauvres. Le Haasenhof (photo ci-dessus) de Magdalena Haase, datant de 1727, est le plus récent d'entre eux. La pièce du président est très décorative. Le Füchtings Hof (à droite) est le plus vaste.

Die Lübecker Bürgerhäuser standen an der Straße dicht an dicht in geschlossener Bauweise. Unten befanden sich die Diele, die Büros, die Küche und auch der Wohnraum, und in den oberen Stockwerken war der Lagerraum. Als der Platz für das Wohnen im Haupthaus nicht mehr ausreichte, entstand nach hinten ein Flügelanbau.

Lübeck's town houses stood side by side on the street in a unified style of construction. Downstairs were the hall, offices, kitchen as well as the living room, and the storeroom was on the upper floors. When the living space in the main building was no longer sufficient, a wing was built onto the rear.

Les maisons des bourgeois de Lübeck étaient construites les unes contre les autres et formaient un ensemble. En bas se trouvaient le vestibule, les bureaux, la cuisine et les autres pièces habitables. Les étages supérieurs servaient d'entrepôts. Lorsque la place devenait insuffisante, on ajoutait une aile vers l'arrière.

Das Heilig-Geist-Hospital ist die älteste soziale Einrichtung Lübecks, die schon nach 1280 entstanden ist. Das dreigiebelige Gebäude wurde um 1286 vollendet und ist die Kirche zu dem dahinter befindlichen Hospital und späteren Altersheim. Das Langhaus mit den vielen Buden, von denen jede früher eine Altenunterkunft war, ist 88 m lang.

The Heilig-Geist Hospital is the oldest social facility in Lübeck, dating from after 1280. The three-gabled building was completed around 1286 and is the church for the hospital situated behind it, later to become an old age home. The nave with the numerous booths, each of which used to offer lodging for the elderly, is 88 m long.

Le Heilig-Geist-Hospital, commencé en 1280, est la plus vieille institution sociale de Lübeck. L'édifice à trois pignons, terminé vers 1286, est l'église de l'hôpital (plus tard asile de vieillards) qui est situé derrière. La nef avec les nombreuses pièces où étaient logés les vieux a 88 m de long.

Die Sanierung der Altstadt ist ein wichtiges Mittel, um die Abwanderung aus Lübeck in das Umland zu stoppen. Dabei geht es darum, sowohl die Räumlichkeiten zu erweitern und mehr Wohnkomfort zu schaffen als auch ein ästhetisches Äußeres wiederherzustellen. Von der Sanierung werden Höfe wie der Glandorps Hof ebenso erfaßt wie das Doppelhaus in der Großen Gröpelgrube.

Renewal of the Old Town is an important means for stopping migration out of Lübeck to the surrounding area. The aim here is to expand the facilities and create more home comfort as well as to restore an aesthetic appearance. The edifices involved in this renewal process include Glandorps Hof and the semi-detached house in Große Gröpelgrube.

L'assainissement des vieux quartiers est un moyen efficace pour retenir les habitants en ville. Pour ceci il faut agrandir les surfaces habitables, apporter plus de comfort et redonner un aspect esthétique à l'extérieur. Le programme d'assainissement inclut les «Höfe» tels que le Glandorps Hof de même que la maison double dans la Große Gröpelgrube.

35

Das Lübecker Burgtor mit seinem markanten Helm ist das einzige erhaltene Stadttor der Hansestadt mit seiner ursprünglichen Funktion. Man verläßt durch dieses Tor die Lübecker Innenstadt nach Norden. Rechts befindet sich das Zöllnerhaus von 1571, in dem die Schriftstellerin Ida Boy-Ed eine Ehrenwohnung von der Stadt gestellt bekam.

The Burgtor in Lübeck with its striking helm roofs is the only intact town gate in the Hanseatic city that still has its original function. One leaves Lübeck's center through this gate heading towards the north. On the right is Zöllnerhaus dating from 1571 where the writer Ida Boy-Ed was given an honorary apartment by the city.

La Burgtor, avec son remarquable sommet est la seule porte fortifiée de la ville hanséatique qui ait été conservée. Par cette porte on quitte, au nord, le centre de la ville. A droite, se trouve la Zöllnerhaus de 1571. La ville honora la femme de lettres Ida Boy-Ed en y mettant un logis à sa disposition.

Das Burgkloster wurde nach dem Sieg gegen Dänemark im Jahre 1227 als gotisches Kloster für die Dominikaner errichtet. Die freigelegte mittelalterliche Malerei befindet sich in der Sakristei. Heute dient das ehemalige Kloster als Museum und Ausstellungseinrichtung. Als Besonderheit wird der sehenswerte große Lübecker Münzschatz gezeigt.

The castle monastery was built for the Dominicans as a Gothic cloister after the victory against Denmark in 1227. The exposed medieval painting work is in the sacristy. Today the former monastery serves as a museum and exhibition site. One of the special exhibits worth seeing is the large Lübeck collection of coins.

Le cloître fut érigé comme cloître gothique pour les Dominicains après la victoire sur le Danemark en 1227. La fresque apparente datant du Moyen-Age se trouve dans la sacristie. De nos jours, l'ancien cloître fait office de musée et de salle d'expositions. A noter, la grande collection de monnaies de Lübeck.

Fritz
Reuter
Eik

Viele Grünzonen umgeben die Hansestadt Lübeck. Neben den Wäldern bieten auch die stadtnahen Parks, z.B. die Wallanlagen, der Dräger- und Stadtpark (links), Erholungsmöglichkeiten.

Der Behnhausgarten ist ein Teil der Bürgergärten der Hansestadt. Links erkennt man das Behnhaus, rechts das Drägerhaus. Beide sind kunst- und kulturgeschichtliche Museen.

Many green areas surround the Hanseatic city of Lübeck. Besides the forests, there are also nearby parks, such as the town embankment grounds, Drägerpark and Stadtpark (on the left), offering recreation and relaxation.

Behnhaus Garden is part of the town gardens of the Hanseatic city. On the left one can see Behnhaus, on the right Drägerhaus. Both are museums of art and cultural history.

De nombreux espaces verts entourent la ville de Lübeck. A proximité de la ville, les forêts, les parcs des Wallanlagen, de Drägerpark et de Stadtpark sont des lieux de détente pour les habitants.

Le Behnhausgarten fait partie des Bürgergärten. A gauche, on reconnaît la Behnhaus, à droite, la Drägerhaus. Toutes deux sont des musées d'histoire de l'art et de la culture.

Von Westen nähert man sich der Hansestadt Lübeck über die Puppenbrücke der historischen Altstadt. Die Originale der Sandsteinfiguren von Dietrich Jürgen Boy von 1774 bis 1776 sind durch Nachbildungen ersetzt worden. Götterbote Merkur wendet den Besuchern den „bloßen Podex“ (E. Geibel) zu.

Zu Lübeck auf der Brücken,
da steht der Gott Merkur.
Er zeigt in allen Stücken
olympische Figur.
Er wußte nichts von Hemden
in seiner Götterruh',
drum kehrt er allen Fremden
den bloßen Podex zu.
(Emanuel Geibel)

From the west one approaches the Hanseatic city of Lübeck via the Puppet Bridge of the historical Old Town. The original sandstone figures created by Dietrich Jürgen Boy from 1774 to 1776 have been replaced by replicas. Mercury, the messenger of the gods, turns his “bare posterior” (E. Geibel) to visitors.

On a bridge in Lübeck,
stands the god, Mercury,
in every way displaying
Olympic stature.
He knew nothing of clothing
in his divine repose,
thus to all passers-by
he turns his bare posterior.
(Emanuel Geibel)

On atteint la ville hanséatique de Lübeck, à l'ouest, par le Puppenbrücke de la vieille ville historique. Les sculptures de grès de D.J. Boy, datant de 1774 à 1776, ont été remplacées par des copies. Le messager des dieux, Mercure, tourne vers les visiteurs son «postérieur nu» (E. Geibel).

A Lübeck, sur le pont,
se trouve le dieu Mercure.
Il montre en tous points
un aspect olympien.
Point ne connaisait de chemise
dans son naturel divin.
Aussi vers tous les étrangers
il tourne son postérieur nu.
(Emanuel Geibel)

Seit dem Mittelalter ist Lübeck von mehreren Sicherungsanlagen umgeben. Neben den natürlichen Sicherungen von Trave und Wakenitz gibt es einen Stadtgraben, die Wallanlagen, die Stadttore, Türme und die Stadtmauer, die im Osten der Stadt nach der Restaurierung zum Teil wieder zu sehen ist.

Since the Middle Ages Lübeck has been surrounded by several protective elements. In addition to the natural protection offered by the Trave and Wakenitz, there is a town moat, embankment, town gates, towers and the city wall that can partially be seen again in the eastern section of the town after restoration.

Depuis le Moyen Age, Lübeck est entourée de nombreuses constructions défensives. En plus des défenses naturelles que constituent la Trave et le Wakenitz, il y a un fossé, des remblais, des portes fortifiées, des tours et des remparts dont on peut voir les vestiges restaurés à l'est de la ville.

Das Statius-von-Düren-Haus befindet sich in der Musterbahn 3. Viele Terrakotten verzieren die Hausfront und lassen etwas von der großen Kunst dieses Handwerks erahnen. Auch an anderen Gebäuden der Altstadt, z.B. am Holstentor und am Zöllnerhaus am Burgtor, sind noch Terrakotten des Statius von Düren erhalten geblieben.

The Statius-von-Düren House is located at Musterbahn 3. Much terracotta work adorns the house-front, giving one an idea of the great art involved in this craft. Terracotta work by Statius von Düren has also remained preserved on other buildings in the Old Town, for example, at Holstentor and at Zöllnerhaus at the Castle Gate.

La Statius-von-Düren-Haus est située au no 3 de la Musterbahn. Des reliefs de terre cuite décorent la façade de la maison et nous donnent un aperçu de la grande valeur artistique de cet artisanat. D'autres bâtiments de la vieille ville, la Holstentor et la Zöllnerhaus de la Burgtor par exemple, sont aussi ornées de reliefs de terre cuite de Statius von Düren.

Das St. Annen-Museum ist ein Museum für Lübecker Kunst- und Kulturgeschichte. Neben zwei Innenhöfen – in einem befinden sich die Originalfiguren der Puppenbrücke – beherbergt der Hauptraum, der Remter, des kurz vor der Reformation entstandenen Klosters, eine umfangreiche Sammlung Lübecker Altäre.

The St. Annen Museum is a museum for Lübeck's art and cultural history. In addition to two inner courtyards – the original figures of the Puppet Bridge are in one of them – the main room, "Remter" (refectory), of the convent dating from shortly before the Reformation, contains an extensive collection of Lübeck altars.

Le St. Annen-Museum est un musée de l'histoire de l'art et de la culture de Lübeck. En plus de deux cours intérieures (dans l'une se trouvent les originaux des sculptures du Puppenbrücke), le Remter, la salle principale de ce monastère fondé peu avant la Réforme, renferme une riche collection d'autels de Lübeck.

Die gotischen Stadtkirchen

Das Lübecker Stadtbild wird durch die einmalige Kirchenlandschaft geprägt, die der Hansestadt die Bezeichnung „Stadt der sieben Türme“ eintrug.
Der Dom ist eine dreischiffige Hallenkirche aus Backstein, mit deren Bau um 1173 begonnen wurde. Die beiden Türme erhielten nach dem Krieg einen neuen Helm. Sehenswert ist das nördliche Vorhallenportal, das sogenannte Paradies, sowie das Triumphkreuz und die Kapellen im südlichen Seitenschiff.

Lübeck's townscape is characterized by the unique church panorama that gave the Hanseatic city the name "city of seven towers".
The cathedral is a three-nave brick church whose construction was begun around 1173. The two towers received a new helm roof after the war. The northern vestibule portal, so-called Paradise, as well as the triumphal cross and the chapels in the southern side aisle are worth viewing.

L'aspect de Lübeck doit beaucoup à ses églises au cachet bien particulier qui lui ont valu d'être nommée «la ville des sept clochers».
La cathédrale est une église de brique à trois vaisseaux dont la construction fut commencée en 1173. Les deux clochers ont été dotés de nouvelles flèches après la guerre. Le portail du narthex nord, appelé «le Paradis», la grande croix d'apparat et la chapelle du bas-côté sud sont remarquables.

Das über 17 m hohe Triumphkreuz im Dom schuf Bernt Notke für den Bischof Albert Krummedik. Mit dem Lettner dahinter bildet es eine besondere Einheit. Man braucht Zeit, um den religiösen Sinn dieses Kunstwerks voll zu entschlüsseln. Eindrucksvoll ist auch die Kanzel von 1568.

Bernt Notke created the over 17 m high triumphal cross in the cathedral for Bishop Albert Krummedik. It forms a special unity with the choir screen behind it. One needs time to decipher the religious meaning of this work of art. The pulpit dating from 1568 is also impressive.

Dans la cathédrale, la grande croix d'apparat de 17 m de haut fut réalisée par Bernt Notke pour l'évêque Albert Krummedik. Elle forme une unité avec le jubé qui se trouve derrière. Il faut longtemps pour bien comprendre la signification religieuse de cette œuvre d'art. La chaire de 1568 est, elle aussi, très impressionnante.

Die Marienkirche zeigt vom Petriturm aus ihre volle Ausdruckskraft als gotische Backsteinhallenkirche. Mit 125 bzw. 126 m Höhe sind die Kirchtürme die höchsten Norddeutschlands. Auch St. Marien wurde in der Palmsonntagnacht 1942 zerstört. Der figurenreiche Marienaltar befindet sich in der Marientidenkapelle.

From the Petri tower the Marienkirche displays its full espressiveness as a Gothic brick church. Having a height of 125 m and 126 m, respectively, the church towers are the highest in northern Germany. St. Marien was also destroyed during Palm Sunday night in 1942. The Altar of the Virgin Mary with its many figures is located in the Marientiden Chapel.

C'est du clocher de la Petrikirche que la Marienkirche manifeste toute sa force d'expression d'église du gothique de brique. Ses clochers de 125 et 126 m sont les plus hauts d'Allemagne du nord. La Marienkirche fut, elle aussi, détruite pendant la nuit du dimanche de Rameaux 1942. L'autel, riche en personnages, se trouve dans la Marientidenkapelle.

Die Petrikirche ist die einzige fünfschiffige Hallenkirche in Norddeutschland. Der gotische Bau mit den hohen spitzbogigen Fenstern läßt nicht erkennen, daß er aus einem romanischen Vorbau entstanden ist. Die ursprünglich dreischiffige Kirche wurde im 15. und 16. Jahrhundert in ein fünfschiffiges Gotteshaus, das sich nach der Restaurierung in einem schlichten Weiß mit wenig Ornamentik zeigt, umgewandelt.

The Petri Church is the only five-nave hall-type church in northern Germany. The Gothic structure with its high, pointed arch windows does not show that it originated from a previous Romanic edifice. In the 15th and 16th century the originally three-nave church was converted into a five-nave house of worship that since its restoration has displayed itself in plain white with little ornamentation.

La Petrikirche est la seule église à cinq vaisseaux d'Allemagne du nord. L'édifice gothique aux hautes ogives ne laisse pas reconnaître qu'il s'est developpé à partir d'une construction romane. L'église qui, à l'origine, avait trois vaisseaux fut remaniée aux 15 et 16e siècles et transformée en édifice blanc, très sobre.

Die Große Orgel in St. Jakobi hat eine über 500 Jahre alte Geschichte und ist ein ausgesprochenes Kunstwerk mit ihrem herrlichen Orgelprospekt. Auch Hugo Distler spielte an diesem Musikinstrument. Sehens- und hörenswert ist ebenfalls die kleine Stellwagenorgel von 1467/1515 an der Nordwand von St. Jakobi.

The Great Organ in St. Jakobi has an over 500-year-old history and is a genuine work of art with its magnificent organ backdrop. Hugo Distler also played on this musical instrument. The small organ on the north wall of St. Jakobi, dating from 1467/1515, is also worth seeing and hearing.

Le grand orgue dans l'église St. Jakobi a plus de 500 ans et est une véritable œuvre d'art avec son magnifique buffet d'orgue. C'est à cet instrument que jouait Hugo Distler. Le petit orgue de 1467/1515, sur le côté nord de St. Jakobi, vaut aussi la peine d'être vu et entendu.

Die Katharinenkirche erhebt sich mit ihrem Chor und den beiden Querschiffen nur wenig über die Dächer der Stadt. Sehenswert sind in der Westfassade dieser Museumskirche die Figuren von Ernst Barlach und Gerhard Marcks. Der reichverzierte Lettner in St. Aegidien ist eine Schnitzarbeit von Tönnies Evers d.J. aus dem Jahre 1587.

Katharinenkirche with its choir and two transepts rises only slightly above the roofs of the city. The figures of Ernst Barlach and Gerhard Marcks in the west facade of this museum church are well worth seeing. The richly ornamented choir screen in St. Aegidien consists of carving work by Tönnies Evers the Younger from the year 1587.

Le chœur et les deux transepts de la Katharinenkirche ne s'élèvent qu'à peine au-dessus des toits de la ville. Sur la façade ouest de cette église transformée en musée, les plastiques d'Ernst Barlach et de Gerhard Marcks sont remarquables. Le jubé richement sculpté dans St. Aegidien est une œuvre de Tönnies Evers le Jeune et date de 1587.

Hafen und Wirtschaft

An der Untertrave zwischen Lübeck und Travemünde hat sich in den letzten 100 Jahren eine Industriegasse entwickelt. Maschinenfabriken, ein Hochofenwerk, ein Kraftwerk, ein keramisches Werk, Stahlhochbau sowie ein Baggerbauunternehmen siedelten sich unter anderem hier an. Sie tragen neben den Schiffswerften beträchtliches zur Wirtschaft Lübecks bei.

An industrial lane has developed on the Lower Trave between Lübeck and Travemünde over the last 100 years. Machine plants, a blast furnace works, a power plant, a ceramics factory, steel building construction firms as well as a power shovel construction company, among others, were established here and along with the shipyards represent an integral part of Lübeck's economy.

Sur la Trave inférieure, entre Lübeck et Travemünde, s'est développé, pendant les cent dernières années, un couloir industriel. Des usines de constructions mécaniques, un haut fourneau, une usine de force motrice, une usine de céramique, une aciérie et une usine de pelles mécaniques se sont installées ici. Ces industries, auxquelles il faut ajouter les chantiers de constructions navales, contribuent à l'économie de Lübeck.

Lübeck – Travemünde

Travemünde, „die schönste Tochter“ der Hansestadt, ist ein Stadtteil an der Lübecker Bucht. Ursprünglich war es eine kleine Fischersiedlung mit dem Zentrum um die St. Lorenzkirche. Zum Fischereihafen, in dessen Nähe regelmäßig ein Fischmarkt veranstaltet wird, haben es die Berufs- und Hobbyfischer nicht weit.

Travemünde, "the most beautiful daughter" of the Hanseatic city, is a city district on Lübeck Bay. Originally it was a small fishing settlement with its center around St. Lorenz Church. The professional and amateur fischermen do not have a long way to get to the Fishery Harbor, in the proximity of which a fish market is held regularly.

Travemünde, «la plus belle fille» de la ville hanséatique est un quartier situé sur la baie de Lübeck. A l'origine c'était un petit village de pêcheurs groupé autour de la St. Lorenzkirche. Les pêcheurs professionnels ou amateurs n'ont pas loin à aller pour rejoindre le port de pêche près duquel a lieu régulièrement un marché aux poissons.

Lübeck ist seit den Tagen der Hansezeit mit der Ostsee verbunden. Schon im Bereich der Travemündung liegen viele kleine und große Fährschiffe, Segelschiffe, Motorboote, Fischkutter und Butterdampfer. Einige dieser Schiffe fahren nur in der Lübecker Bucht, andere verbinden die Fährhäfen der Ostseeanrainerstaaten. Der Dampfschiff- Eisbrecher Stettin – heute ein Museumsschiff – liegt als besondere Attraktion an der Travemündung.

Lübeck has been attached to the Baltic Sea since the days of the Hanseatic League. In the area around the mouth of the Trave there are many small and large ferry boats, sailboats, motor boats, fishing cutters and so-called “butter” steamships. Some of these boats only sail in Lübeck Bay, others connect the ferry ports of the countries bordering the Baltic Sea. The steamship- icebreaker Stettin – today a museum ship – lies at anchor at the mouth of the Trave as a special attraction.

Depuis le temps de la Hanse, Lübeck est liée à la mer Baltique. A l’embouchure de la Trave se trouvent de nombreux bacs petits et grands, des voiliers, des bateaux à moteur, des cotres et des vapeurs. Les uns ne circulent que dans la baie de Lübeck, d’autres relient les ports de ferry de la Baltique les uns aux autres. Le brise-glaces à vapeur Stettin – aujourd’hui musée – est une attraction toute spéciale à l’embouchure de la Trave.

Aus dem kleinen Fischerdorf Travemünde ist mit Lübeck zusammen der größte Fährhafen Europas geworden. Von dem seit 1962 sich entwickelnden Skandinavienkai wird der gesamte Personen- und Autoverkehr in die nordischen Länder abgewickelt. Circa 670000 Passagiere werden von hier aus befördert, unter anderem von der Finnjet, dem größten Travemünde regelmäßig anlaufenden Fährschiff.

Together with Lübeck the small fishing village of Travemünde has become Europe's largest ferry port. The entire passenger and rolling traffic bound for the Nordic countries is handled at Skandinavienkai, which has been developing since 1962. Approximately 670000 passengers are transported from here, on the Finnjet, for example, the largest ferry regularly sailing to and from Travemünde.

L'ancien petit village de pêcheurs de Travemünde est devenu, joint à la ville de Lübeck, le plus grand port de ferry d'Europe. Du Skandinavienkai qui date de 1962, s'effectue la totalité du transport de personnes et de véhicules avec les pays nordiques. Près de 670000 de passagers sont transportés de cet endroit par le «Finnjet», en particulier, le plus grand ferry en service régulier à Travemünde.

Travemünde entwickelte sich seit 1802 zu einem Ostseeheilbad an der inneren Lübecker Bucht. Wasser, Strand, Kurpromenade, Kurgarten, ein Meerwasser-Wellenbad, ein Kurmittelhaus sowie andere Einrichtungen laden zum Erholen und Heilen ein. Das international bekannte Heilbad hat eine ganzjährige Saison. Links unten im Bild erkennt man das Casino.

Since 1802 Travemünde has developed into a Baltic Sea spa on the inner coast of Lübeck Bay. Water, beach, promenade, spa garden, a seawater swimming pool with artificially induced waves, spa rooms as well as other facilities are inviting for relaxation and healing purposes. The internationally known spa is open all year round. On the bottom left of the picture one can see the casino.

Depuis 1802, Travemünde est devenu une ville de bains de mer sur la baie de Lübeck. L'eau, le sable, les promenades, le jardin, une piscine d'eau de mer avec des vagues, un établissement balnéaire et d'autres facilités invitent au repos et à la guérison. Cette station balnéaire, connue dans le monde entier, accueille les curistes toute l'année. En bas à gauche, dans la photo, on reconnaît le casino.

Die Passat liegt an der Travemündung auf der Priwallseite fest. Dieser P-Liner erinnert an die Zeit der großen Segelschiffe, die einst die Weltmeere befuhren. Heute ist das „Museumsschiff“ für die Öffentlichkeit zugänglich. Die Passat wird immer mehr das Symbol für die Travemünder Woche.

The Passat is tied up on the Priwall side of the mouth of the Trave. This P-liner reminds one of the times of the large sailing ships that once sailed the open seas. Today the "Museum Ship" is open to the public. The Passat will always be the symbol for Travemünde Week.

Le Passat est ancré dans la baie de Lübeck sur la rive de Priwall. Ce «P-Liner» rappelle le temps des grands voiliers qui voguaient, jadis, sur les mers du globe. C'est aujourd'hui un bateau musée ouvert au public. Le Passat est devenu le symbole de la semaine de Travemünde.

Chronik

819
Nachweis der Siedlung und Burganlage Alt Lübeck am Zusammenfluß von Trave und Schwartau.
1138
Zerstörung der christlichen Siedlung Alt Lübeck durch heidnische Wenden.
1143
Gründung Lübecks durch Graf Adolf II. von Holstein auf dem Hügel zwischen Wakenitz und Trave.
1157
Neugründung Lübecks an der Wakenitz durch Heinrich den Löwen nach einer Feuersbrunst.
1159
Erneute Gründung Lübecks am heutigen Marktplatz.
1160
Verlegung des Bischofssitzes von Oldenburg/Holstein nach Lübeck. Bald danach Beginn der Kirchenbauten.
1181
Bestätigung und Erweiterung von Privilegien durch Kaiser Friedrich Barbarossa.
1226
Verleihung der Reichsfreiheit durch Kaiser Friedrich II.
1251/76
Die Vernichtung großer Teile Lübecks durch Feuer führt zur Ausbreitung der Backsteinbauweise.
1358
Urkundliche Belegung der Bezeichnung „Städte von der deutschen Hanse". Lübeck entwickelt sich zum Haupt dieses Handelsbündnisses und geht als Königin der Hanse in die Geschichte ein.
1529/30
Reformation in Lübeck.
1621/41
Errichtung der Wallanlagen als Stadtbefestigung.
1630
Letzter Hansetag in Lübeck. Lübeck, Hamburg und Bremen tragen weiter die Bezeichnung Hansestadt.
1806
Besetzung der Stadt durch französische Truppen. Bis 1813 gehört Lübeck zum französischen Kaiserreich.
1815
Mitglied im Deutschen Bund.
1866
Beitritt zum Norddeutschen Bund.
1871
Lübeck wird Gliedstaat im Deutschen Reich.
1900
Einweihung des Elbe-Lübeck-Kanals.
1937
Eingliederung in die preußische Provinz Schleswig-Holstein und Ende der Reichsfreiheit nach 711 Jahren.
ab 1962
Entwicklung zum größten Fährhafen Europas und Tor nach Skandinavien durch den Skandinavienkai in Travemünde.
1987
Anerkennung als Weltkulturgut durch die UNESCO.
1989
100 Jahre Travemünder Woche mit Großseglertreffen.
1993
850-Jahr-Feier der Gründung Lübecks.
Eröffnung des Heinrich- und Thomas-Mann-Zentrums im Buddenbrookhaus.
1994
Eröffnung der Musik- und Kongreßhalle (MUK).

Chronicle

819
Vertification of the settlement and castle complex of Alt Lübeck at confluence of Trave and Schwartau.
1138
Destruction of Christian settlement of Alt Lübeck by heathen Wends.
1143
Lübeck is founded by Count Adolf II von Holstein on the hill between Wakenitz and Trave.
1157
Re-establishment of Lübeck on Wakenitz by Heinrich der Löwe after outbreak of fire.
1159
Lübeck re-established at present marketplace.
1160
Transfer of diocesan seat from Oldenburg/Holstein to Lübeck. Soon thereafter beginning of church building.
1181
Confirmation and expansion of privileges by Kaiser Friedrich Barbarossa.
1226
Conferring of status of free city by Kaiser Friedrich II.
1251/76
Destruction of large parts of Lübeck by fire leads to spread of brickwork architecture.
1358
Documentary proof of designation "cities of the German Hanseatic League". Lübeck develops into head of this trade alliance and goes down in history as queen of the Hanseatic League.
1529/30
Reformation in Lübeck.
1621/41
Setting up of embankment as city fortifications.
1630
Last Hanseatic conference in Lübeck. Lübeck, Hamburg and Bremen continue to bear the designation Hanseatic city.
1806
Occupation of the city by French troops. Until 1813 Lübeck belongs to French Empire.
1815
Member of German Confederation.
1866
Joins Northern German Confederation.
1871
Lübeck becomes member state in German Empire.
1900
Official opening of Elbe-Lübeck Canal.
1937
Incorporation into Prussian province of Schleswig-Holstein and end of status of free city after 711 years.
As of 1962
Development into largest ferry port in Europe and gateway to Scandinavia via Skandinavienkai in Travemünde.
1987
Recognition as international cultural asset by UNESCO.
1989
100 years of Travemünde Week with gathering of large sailing ships.
1993
850th anniversary of the founding of Lübeck.
Opening of Heinrich and Thomas Mann Center in Buddenbrook House.
1994
Opening of Music and Convention Hall (MUK).

Histoire

819
Une colonie de peuplement et un fort – Alt Lübeck – existent au confluent de la Trave et de la Schwartau.
1138
La colonie chrétienne d'Alt Lübeck est détruite par les Wendes païens.
1143
Fondation de Lübeck par le comte Adolf II von Holstein sur la colline entre la Wakenitz et la Trave.
1157
Après un incendie, Lübeck est fondé de nouveau sur la Wakenitz par Henri le Lion.
1159
Lübeck est fondé de nouveau sur l'emplacement de la place du Marché.
1160
Le siège de l'épiscopat est déplacé d'Oldenburg/Holstein à Lübeck. La construction des églises suit peu après.
1181
L'empereur Frédéric Barberousse confirme et étend les privilèges de la ville.
1226
L'empereur Frédéric II accorde à Lübeck le privilège de ville libre impériale.
1251/76
Des incendies détruisent plusieurs quartiers de la ville. Les constructions de brique deviennent plus nombreuses.
1358
L'appellation «villes de la Hanse allemande» mentionnée dans les documents. Lübeck devient la capitale de cette alliance commerciale et passe à l'histoire comme reine de la Hanse.
1529/30
La Réforme à Lübeck.
1621/41
Construction des remparts.
1630
Dernière assemblée de la Hanse à Lübeck. Lübeck, Hambourg et Brême continuent à porter le titre de «ville hanséatique».
1806
Occupation de la ville par les troupes françaises. La ville fait partie de l'Empire Français jusqu'en 1813.
1815
Lübeck est membre de la Ligue Allemande.
1866
Lübeck est membre de la Ligue d'Allemagne du nord.
1871
Lübeck est un état membre de l'Empire Allemand.
1900
Inauguration du canal Elbe-Lübeck.
1937
La ville est incorporée à la province prussienne de Schleswig-Holstein. Fin de la libertè impériale après 711 ans.
A partir de 1962
Lübeck devient le plus grand port de ferry d'Europe et une porte sur la Scandinavie après la construction du Skandinavienkai à Travemünde.
1987
La ville est reconnue bien culturel mondial par l'UNESCO.
1989
Centenaire de la semaine de Travemünde avec grande rencontre de voiliers.
1993
850e anniversaire de la ville de Lübeck.
Inauguration de Centre Heinrich et Thomas Mann dans la «Buddenbrookhaus».
1994
Inauguration du Palais de la Musique et des Congrès (MUK).